I Changed My Name

I Changed My Name

Jerry Harris Moore
&
Michael McCranie

Red Engine Press
Fort Smith, Arkansas

Copyright © 2026 Jerry Moore and Michael McCranie

ALL RIGHTS RESERVED. No part of this book may be reproduced or transmitted in any form or by any means, electronic or mechanical, including photocopying, recording, or by any information storage and retrieval system (except by a reviewer or commentator who may quote brief passages in a printed or on-line review) without permission of the publisher.

Cover Design by Joyce Faulkner

Library of Congress Control Number: 2026930736

ISBN: 979-8-9985192-1-5

Material from Harris, Moore, Martin, and Walker Families Collection housed at the University of Arkansas Special Collection Department, Fayetteville, Arkansas is the source for much of this work.

In Memory of Doyle and Eva Moore, Jerry Harris Sr., Darlene Moore Harris Fletcher, Douglass Fletcher, Allen Fletcher, Donnell Fletcher and Eugene Ferro

Dedicated to Alice Faye Johnson Vege, Scott William Davis and my Upward Bound Students

Alice Faye has always been my best friend. Our parents put us together at a young age, and we were more like brother and sister than friends down the street. Her parents were close to my grandparents that I grew up with. Each of us was the others support mechanism for many years.

The other person I have dedicated this personal testament to is Scott William Davis of Paris, Arkansas. Scott was assigned to look after me, as a favor via Bill Clinton as he was transitioning to his first term as President of the United States. Although I knew Scott's family, I would later learn his background and how it applied to Bill making that request; there is always a basis. Mr. Davis always felt it to be a true honor, as he had not voted Democrat, and it has been customary to bring along those friendly to the Party. Mr. Davis would have accompanied me had I accepted the position offered by Bill Clinton in his administration. I just loved teaching and staying here as a teacher was my decision.

I dedicated this to my Upward Bound students as well. You will understand my reason for this honor as you read chapter eight of the book.

Table of Contents

PREFACE VI

CHAPTER 1 — FROM KANSAS CITY, KANSAS TO HUNTINGTON, ARKANSAS 1

CHAPTER 2 — THAT SEPTEMBER 9, 1952, VISIT TO THE POST OFFICE AND AFTER 10

CHAPTER 3 — MY EARLY EDUCATIONAL JOURNEY ..18

CHAPTER 4 — BUS ONE 25

CHAPTER 5 — BEACON OF HOPE 35

CHAPTER 6 — NEW CHALLENGES AHEAD 50

CHAPTER 7 — SIX TWENTY-NINE NORTH LINDELL ...65

CHAPTER 8 — UPWARD FOCUS 77

CHAPTER 9 — THE PERSON I SEE IN THE MIRROR 88

IMAGES OF MY LIFE 98

Preface

In the next few pages, I will share some of my life with you. In the last ten years or so many people asked me to write about my experiences. I kept telling them that my life is not important to anyone else but me. I felt that my life was personal, so I did not share it publicly with my childhood friends until now.

I selected stories in my life that would be a learning experience for those who would read it. You will get what I can remember that will not be offensive to anyone from my past or part of my present. I did not share stories of those who were not comfortable doing an interview for the book, so I honored them by not including them, yet they had a great impact upon my life, and I love them for that.

What remained in my consciousness and mindset was that my life is what it is because I have a Savior, and each day I feel safe in the arms of Jesus.

Read this book with an open mind whether you know me or not.

I Changed My Name!!!!!!!

Chapter 1 — From Kansas City, Kansas to Huntington, Arkansas

Join me as I share with you my life story, a journey that will force me to reflect on past events that may be hard to bring to the forefront within these pages. At times you may think that I am not writing in a timeline method as my life unfolded. But as you finish your reading it will all make sense.

Why should a person want to read about me? I grew up in a small town in Western Arkansas...Huntington. A town that is not known by many in Arkansas or out of state. But maybe this book will introduce my hometown and what it was like growing up there, and how the town prepared me for the life I have had and the effect it had on my development.

For about ten years or more, those I have interacted with have said to me you must write about the stories and experiences you have experienced during your life. At first it was hard for me to see the impact that my life had on people early in my life to the present. Maybe it was because my hometown, Huntington, was not known to be a Sundown Town in Western Arkansas. That means that Blacks were not allowed in town after sundown. I am sure that my town's leading economic source was coal mining that included all races of worker. The 1910 census of Huntington showed a town population of seventeen hundred with a Black population of two hundred seventy (twenty-two percent of the population) at the height of the coal mining boom. This number of Blacks was about one hundred households.

The center of the Arkansas Socialist Party was in Huntington. The newspaper, the *Herald*, had as its editor and publisher the President of the Arkansas Socialist Party, Dan Hogan. He, along with his daughter and the party, played a vital role in the day-to-day activities of the town. The party would play a major role in the 1914 Coal Riot in which troops were called out to protect the people.

This socialist background of Huntington influenced our views of society by those of us raised in Huntington. Speaking just for me, growing up in this town affected my reactions, opinions, values, morals, and belief system. I think this has made me more open in dealing with others and how I would deal with issues. In many ways it opens doors for me to be present at the table where decisions are made.

What I experienced each day in Huntington was a training ground which affected the self I developed and that impacted who I am today at the age of seventy-four.

I think that I started this self-development as early as twelve-years-old, the age of reason for most. But let me inject this major point I think is very important in telling my story, my birth came early in the seventh month. Maybe I am saying I had a quick start on this earth and my thinking is that I have been ahead in many more ways than others. This early birth was not a disability, a situation that I rebuked in my grade school years and forward.

Next came to mind why thinking about this writing process was what would I talk about or not talk about. Many will not know me, but there will be many who would know me or of me in many cases. I must bring into reality that my family, childhood friends, classmates, people I worked with, and even went to church with all these years will be reading this book.

By this time, I was quickly becoming not that private person that I wanted others to see me as. So, as I write this book, I must focus on the main thought that this book is not for personal gratification but sharing with others my unusual story and let them know that my contributions thus far shaped me into the person that other see me as, the same person I see in my looking glass when I interact with them.

Finally, I concluded that I had a different story to tell. So, I decided to jump into this writing. I am different, not just by race or gender but who I am. The self that so many see is special in so many ways. My experiences over the years and how I have interacted with people whether based on status, roles, race, gender, values, beliefs, are those with certain privileges is a story that is centered around me, and I must tell the story.

I think that my personality played a part in how people reacted with me. I did not hold back when I felt that I would approach someone I did not know but I wanted to know. This trait of forthrightness did open doors at that time and later down the road. I was very cautious when I started this practice. If it became a negative experience I would move on and try it on someone else. I did have some negative reactions to me saying hello to a stranger.

It was always a great joy to go with my grandmother when she went shopping in Fort Smith. We would leave on an early bus from Huntington to Fort Smith and return on the three P.M. bus that would stop in Huntington. These trips were during the late fifties and early sixties. I recall that one day on such a trip we were in the Hunts Department Store on Garrison Avenue in Fort Smith. I saw this older gentleman in the store's basement, and he looked very important, so guess what, I made my move.

"Hello, my name is Jerry, and I live in Huntington. Do you know where that is?"

"Yes." he said.

"What is your name sir?"

"My name is Mr. Hunt."

"So, this is your store?"

"Yes." he said.

I don't remember what we talked about. But each time I went back to that store I would look for him. But if he was talking to someone, I would just wave at him and move on in the store. But when I could talk to him, I enjoyed it. This meant so much to me. In 1972 or 1973 while teaching at Northside High School, one of my students told me that she was Mr. Hunt's granddaughter, and I shared with her the conversations that I would have with him. She returned sometime later and told me that he remembered me and what effect it had on him. That little Black boy became his granddaughter's teacher.

Later I used the same process at the Boston Store on Garrison Avenue. I said let me try this very important gentleman coming toward me.

"Hello, do you work here?"

"Yes, I own the store, and my name is Mr. Nye."

I told him that I live in Huntington. On another visit Mr. Nye saw me and he said, "come with me." We went upstairs to the second floor to a little sandwich shop, and he gave me a sandwich and a drink, don't know about anything sweet. I did not tell my grandmother about either situation. She could have gotten into trouble because Black's were not allowed into the shop. I went only when he took me up there, never on my own. In 1969 and 1970 I worked at a nursing home… Sparks Manor in Fort Smith. One of the nurses working there one evening was named Nurse Nye, Mr. Nye's daughter-in-law. I shared with her my experience with him. I don't remember her reaction.

Again, I was out of my safety zone that I felt I had in Huntington. To this day I still cannot share with you why I did this and how these two important men were really doing for me that was not an acceptance action toward a Black person at that time. I did not feel special, and I did not overdo it at any time. I looked forward to seeing them.

By being raised in a society of many culture war issues, economic and racial inequalities, unfair justice practices, and White Privilege my actions were not normal. I was interacting in uncharted waters for the time. Is it better today than it was then? My personal interaction has not changed, but it seems that it may still exist across the country like it was in the 50s. Why was I able to not let those social barriers stop me as I built some very important relationships in years ahead.

It was on April 26, 1949, at the University of Kansas Medical Center at thirty-nineth and Rainbow, Kansas City, Kansas upon the birth of a little Black boy to Darlene and Jerry Harris that my story begins. I grew up with people telling me that I was special because I was born in the seventh month. Ahead of time, you might say.

This young twenty-year-old girl named this boy Jerry Jr. after his father. This name will become very important in my life down the road.

Like most things in life, it just happens. Nine months after my birth my father died of tuberculosis at the age of twenty-two. He would not have the opportunity to be active in my upbringing. I was robbed of knowing him as well. Mommy did not talk about him very much. She would say he died. This silence will be broken at the age of thirty-five when I had the opportunity to meet his aunts and uncles. More about this later in the chapter.

Things became hard for Mommy. She had two children and within seven months she had her third child. Things became hard for her to support us, even with the help of her sisters. She soon had to decide about her situation and our survival. After a few months she took my older sister Charlette, and me to her parents Doyle and Eva Moore, that lived in Huntington, Arkansas. We went to the house of Mommy's birth. About two years later my sister was returned to Mommy due to the medical condition my sister was born with. She returned to Kansas City so she could get the care she needed. But I stayed with them until their deaths. I was able to give them the care they needed as they aged like they gave to me. I always had the opportunity to go back to Mommy, but I made the right choice to never leave them.

Mommy in 1951, she remarried. Douglass Fletcher became her husband, but to me he was not my stepfather. I respected him as my Mommy's husband. We had a good relationship, for he understood my decision to stay in Huntington.

But you may be asking yourself did Jerry know his real Mother? My grandparents told me for the time I would understand that Darlene was my mother. They did not keep it a secret why I had to come to live with them. They did not know much about my dad, Jerry. So, he became a mystery person from that point forward. My journey through life would be to search for this person and solve this mystery, if this was a real person. At times I would think that Mommy had me by a stranger, and I would never know my dad. As I grew older, I put into action various plans.

The more interaction I had with my Mommy in the years ahead, during Christmas time and special visits led me to know her more and I felt the nature need to really love her. That love got stronger each time I was in her presence. But the love for my Grandparents was just as strong. I had enough love to go around, and they took really good care of me.

Let's skip ahead to the time that I instituted a plan that worked in finding my dad's relatives. It was in 1984, while visiting my Mommy that my older sister told me about meeting a lady at a church in Kansas City, Kansas one Sunday at a singing program and she said that she was my Father's Aunt. They exchanged phone numbers, and she later gave the number to me. I had something that I could do as a follow-up. I sent a letter to her and introduced myself. Time went by without any reply. So, I made a phone call to that Great Aunt and told her that I would be in Kansas City for the Christmas holiday visiting my Mommy and I would like to meet her, if that was okay with her. I gave her my phone number and she called, and we scheduled a day and time. I did not tell my Mommy until I arrived in Kansas City, for I wanted to tell her face to face. Facial expressions will tell me so much more. Mommy did not know that I was researching for his family. My degrees in History and Sociology would not be wasted.

December 23, 1984, I arrived at my Great Aunt's house. I had never seen this lady till then, I was a few months old I guess when she last saw me. I knocked on the door. This lady opens the door, she quickly becomes emotionally uncontrollable. She said, come in please. I entered the house, and there sat this guy. He could not move for a few minutes. He told me that he was my Great Uncle Buddy. The Aunt told me that her name was Aunt Virginia. They both said that I looked like my Dad so much. We talked for several hours. She told me my grandmother's name was Meliva Powell and my grandfather was Arthur Harris. She said that my dad was born on May 22, 1927, in Clearview, Ok. The hometown of the Harris and Powell families. I could not wait to visit that town, and I did a few months later. No one in that town would know me. There is only one person today that lives there that I have met and do talk with on a regular basis. No Harris or Powell relative is in Clearview. I did visit Arthur's grave and got a death announcement.

She had no picture of Jerry but the last letter he wrote to her on December 17, 1949. I read the letter with tears in my eyes. I did not get that letter at that time, but I would about a year later. On that visit she told me the name of the cemetery that my dad was buried at in Kansas City, Kansas. I will discuss that grave visit later.

We then left her house to go and visit another Great Aunt and Uncle. Same reaction at both houses. At our last stop all my Great Aunts and Uncle were with their oldest Great Nephew. I forgot to tell you that Mommy refused to go with me on that visit and other visits with them.

My interaction with my new family became stronger for I was no longer an outsider, but now part of that family forever. Today, all four people I met on that day are no longer with us. I do talk to one of their children monthly. I have been able to share my research information that they do not know or have. A day that I will never forget.

Let me turn to the story about visiting my dad's grave. A little background about how I came to do this visit. On several occasions I would go over to my Uncle Pepper's house. At the end of the street he lived on was a cemetery. I would run down to the back fence and climb upon it. For a short period of time, I would talk as if my Dad was buried in that place. That gave me some comfort, because I had the opportunity to visit both of my biological parents, one living and the other dead. Remember the visit to my Dad's Aunt she told me about the cemetery he was buried in there in Kansas City, Kansas. So, I called the City Parks and Cemeteries Department to ask questions. I told the person the name of the cemetery was Woodland. They ask when I would like to go there with them. I scheduled a June 1985 date. When I arrived at my Mommy's house the next day I called and told the person at that department that I was in town, and I could meet them on Saturday around one

P.M. I arrived and they were there. The person showed me a map of the area that his grave could be. The same place where I would visit and sit on the fence. I started my walking and all at once I stepped on a grave. I began to cry and shake all over, unable to move I started to scream, and the person came over with the map, and it was Jerry's grave. I went and got a marker for the grave because I already had the information for it. I returned to the grave and put it there. It came to me that the next day was Father's Day. What can I say!

I rushed back to my Mommy's place, and I told her what I did. All at once her memory came to her about the location. A location that all those years she did not share with me. The mystery was addressed to me. So, from that time forward I could think about what generic traits he had given to me at birth. As I read his letter each night before bed and saw it throughout the day, I know that some of personality traits must be like his. This year while on a zoom meeting with my Monday and Friday group a name of my Dad's Grandfather McGuire came into the meeting. I questioned this person, and she said that she would talk to her mother and give her my contact information so we could talk to each other. The contact was made, and this person is three years younger than my Dad and they grew up together for a short period of time in Kansas City, Kansas but her older brother was Jerry's best friend, and she described my Dad to me, and I sent her a picture of me and told me that I looked like him, but he was a little lighter in skin color. Again, a person that knew him. Each time we talk it means so much to me.

The next chapter may seem out of place, but I am writing mainly around experiences in my life that shaped the self that I became over the years. Thinking also about what my life would be like with him, there to share and assist in those experiences. He was not, and I still survived.

Chapter 2 — That September 9, 1952, Visit to the Post Office and After

Today seventy-one years ago I had a car accident in front of the Huntington Post Office. This reflection is based on what I remember and what my grandparent told me. What happened that day has been retold for years by others living in Huntington on that day.

It was early in the morning. I woke up and ran to the kitchen and ask my grandmother, where is Uncle Joe going? She told me that he was taking my grandfather and other men to the cemetery to dig a grave for a funeral that day. My grandmother told me that I needed to eat and get dressed and that I could go with Uncle Joe later to the Post Office. I ate and got ready waiting for him to return.

Uncle Joe returned, but it was later that he told me that he was ready. I ran to the car, and we were on our way to the Post Office. We stopped and picked up a neighbor who would ride with us. We got to the Post Office, and I got out of the driver's side of the car. Into the Post Office we went. We soon returned to the car, and I got on the driver's side. I stood next to Uncle Joe. What happened next has always been clear to me. As the car was put into reverse, I lost my balance and fell against the passenger door, and it was not closed completely. My grandparents related to me that I fell out of the car, and it ran over the left side of my head, cutting the top part of my left ear and all the top skin above the ear to my skull. Uncle Joe said that he soon knew that he had hit me. He picked me up from the ground, held the hanging part of my ear to my head and ran to the doctor's office four doors away. In a few weeks he showed me where I bled from the Post Office to the doctor's office upon the sidewalk. I can be truthful that my blood is on the sidewalk of my hometown. The sidewalk on that day is still the same. It has not been replaced. From that time forward I walked on my blood that was embedded on the sidewalk. Two months ago, I walked again on that sidewalk and hope to do it again for many years ahead. Each September, if I could, I returned to the spot reacting to the event each time.

To save my life I had to be taken to Dr. Wood's Office because the nearest hospital was in Fort Smith, which had separate hospitals based on race. This happened in Huntington, one of the most diverse towns in Western Arkansas. Dr. G.G. Wood and his son Dr. Merle Wood went to work to save my life. You see many white doctors in the South would not serve Blacks. But in Huntington it was different though it had segregated practices and racist people as well. Our churches and schools were segregated but I cannot recall seeing any Jim Crow signs around town. The makeup of Huntington's population was based on the top economic source of coal that established the Coal Mines and its workers who included Blacks, Whites, Mexicans, Italians, Germans, Dutch, Czechoslovakians, Yugoslavians, Irish, Welsh, and Catholics. Strong relationships were built between the people to the community. Even though the city was divided by a creek that separated the coal mine area from the business areas, no established Black and White section of town existed.

I can clearly recall that I looked up while on the table and saw all those people standing around me. My grandmother told me that Dr. Woods laid me back down on the table to complete the operation.

My grandparents took me home and put me to bed. Grandmother called Kansas City to tell the family about the accident. At that time she was told that my Mommy was in labor at the same hospital that I was born in, having a new baby. She had a little girl. Mommy could not come to Huntington for some time to see me. Since that day as my sister celebrates her September ninth Birthday, we talk to each other remembering both events.

Doing the late hours of the night my grandmother told me that I woke up from sleep and began to sing these words "There will be peace in the valley for me someday" by Red Foley that was released on February 27, 1951. She was assured that I had survived the accident.

The support that my Grandparents had from the community helped us to continue. God had other plans for me on this earth. This detour in my early years must have been a sign to me that I would have other detours and barriers to overcome but I will remove them and push forward.

But I like to think that I fought for my life so I could play with my childhood playmates Alice Faye Johnson and Charles Lloyd Repass. Our families were close to each other with a strong bond between them. For your understanding, but not a big deal for me is that Alice Faye was this sweet Black girl with red hair and Charles Llyod was this White boy that grew up loving motorcycles.

What makes a rocky task is that it is the first time I have had to talk about my childhood friends that assisted in my development. I interacted with others, but I was around Alice Faye and Charles more on a one-to-one connectivity. I cannot recall every situation, but I will select a few that had an impact on all three of us.

One thing I can say is that Alice Faye and I spent a lot of time together and I can't say that we were never mad at each other or had harsh words between us. I am sure that it could have happened. She was a little bossy, but I loved her too much to go against her. We were very competitive when it came to learning our ABC and Numbers, speeches at the church for Christmas, Easter,

Mother Day, and Father Day programs. I would act like I did not know my speech before the Sunday Program because I did not want her to correct me, and she would make sure that I would say it correctly like she would do her speech. I went to the front of the church and did it my way with drama!!!

One Christmas I got a doctor's kit, and she got a nurse's kit. We soon understood that my grandparents and her parent may have been hinting something in our future. We kept our friendship like those shared by a sister and brother.

We got our first tricycles at the same time and then our bicycles. On the tricycles we rode them in the pole yard of the electric company across from her house. Since we were older when we got the bicycles, we went all over town for hours. We never dated, per say as teenagers because we did not have a car. When I was of driving age, she was no longer at home since she was about two years old than me.

Time came that Alice Faye was with her first child. After she told her parent, Ms. Ada, her mother, told my grandmother about her situation one day while visiting her. I came out of my room and said in a loud voice, "It is not mine!!!" I talked to her about her having a baby and how it felt. I took on the job of helping her through this process. It was a very happy time of my life. The baby arrived, a little girl. She was so beautiful and still is to this day. I have kept in contact with both from that period until this day. I saw them three weeks ago at Alice Faye's taped interview. I am sure that much more could have been written about our relationship. Maybe there is enough here to recall that really mattered to the both of us.

My other childhood friend Charles Lloyd Repass was the son of our next-door neighbor, the Repass's. This family had a German background. My grandfather grew up around Ms. Repass (Huffman), older brothers, and sisters just North of Huntington.

I came up knowing them as well. In some small way they two had some effects on my development due to these interactions I had with them around town. Both postal workers in the early sixties had married into the Huffman family.

What made our interaction possible was that his mother took care of me when my grandmother had to go somewhere and I did not need to follow, so I went to their house. I guess you could say that Mrs. Repass was my Nanny in some way. I loved her so much. On my last visit with her at the nursing home, as well as other visits that I had with her, I could feel her love and spiritual warmth that she also gave out when I was around her. I made her laugh because she never forgot who I was.

Charles and I played typical boy games and went on long walks among the strip pits near our houses. We had childhood illnesses at the same time. I saw him as an older brother. As we became older and he started working, we spent less time together. He grew up around cars and motorcycles that soon took more time away from our time together. I did not pick up a love for mechanics. Many times, and no matter the time of the day or night, he would ride his motorcycle by my house making all kinds of noise. Even though he soon left home we had some contact with each other in the years ahead until his death.

We had a big yard that became the softball field for the neighborhood. Both the young and old played for hours. Also, our front porch served as the stage where we put our TV set so those who did not have a TV set could come by and watch it. Boy, the conversations shared were very enjoyable at times. I don't recall most of them.

Huntington, Arkansas was divided geographically by Cherokee Creek. The town did not have racial community sections. The town was divided based on how the town was laid out because of the creek. You see, the business sections as well as neighborhoods were East of the creek and the coal mines laid under the city West of the creek. Many towns across the United States were racially divided by a street or railroad tracks but our creek was not like this. I fully believe this; it is because I want to think I am correct, and it helps to tell my story.

Let me make it clear, Jim Crow and Racism was not absent in Huntington. It was there but exhibited differently to fit the community tone of their town as a non-Sundown Town located among others that were Sundown Towns in Western Arkansas.

I gained peace surrounded by the coal strip mines in our backyard. At the bottom of these high hills made from the topsoil from the stripping were pathways that I used to go to the little store south of our house, a quick way to and from my peaceful place. As I walked, or ran if I stayed at the store too long talking to Mr. Columbus, I saw animals, snakes, rabbits, birds, and various vegetation that seemed important to observe, and learned a little about nature. Also, I knew all the poke salad fields where I would pick for my grandmother.

One day on my way to the store, I went around a little turn on the path and as I got closer to the turn and a group of bushes, I began to hear what seemed like voices and the bush shook, I thought. I looked but saw nothing inside the bush. What a weird feeling came over me. I ran on to the store because I couldn't wait to return to see what happened. On my return I heard no voice nor saw the shaking of the bush. At night I would look out of my bedroom window and sometimes I would see people walking and talking toward the strip pit. Maybe it was one of those people hiding in the bushes. I did not discuss this with anyone, especially Alice Faye and

Charles. I would not even tell my grandparents. I did not want to think that my accident caused me to hear voices and see things moving that I could not explain. Who would believe me anyway?

A few months later after this event, our Sunday School lesson taught at Arnett Chapel African Methodist Episcopal in Huntington by Aunt Ruth Johnson was about "Moses and the Burning Bush." I reflected on the strip pit event, and I began to think that it was a sign to me. The event pushed me to the altar on the first Sunday in July 1960 when I joined the church. I was baptized at the altar in the church where my great-grandfather had helped build in 1892 and where my grandfather, grandparents and my Mommy were baptized. I still did not tell anyone about the strip pit calling.

On a visit to a friend in Huntington in 2011 during Christmas Time, Tommie said in our discussion, "Jerry you should have seen the look on your face that day I hid in the bushes in the strip pits and made those voices and shook the bush." I could not believe after all those years that he did that to me. I sat quietly and could not say a word. I then came to reality and told him that I did not know it was him but until that point, I thought it was a spiritual sign to me. He and his wife laughed because she also knew about it. I had to get back somehow so I said, "I have seen other things by those bushes in those strip pits, but I will tell you what I saw, I will keep to myself." They did not have to say anything, reactions were my answer.

I was so lucky to have so many people supporting me. I can't share all my stories. So many trusted me and had respect for me. I will keep some stories for another writing and not this one.

The trust that I gained and shared with so many was very selective. My safety zone was well defined as well. I knew my place. I was able to move among the city at ease making sure I did not go to any uncomfortable areas. My grandfather was very protective of me. I did not want him to have to confront anyone, for it would not be a great sight to see or hear. He taught me to act as dumb as others thought I looked and not speak without listening first so I could make sure that when I spoke the other people were the dumbest, a skill that paid off in the years ahead. I would not be in Huntington my entire life, so I needed the skills my grandparents helped me to develop as I matured into manhood. When I arrived at that stage in my life, I was ready. It is hard to realize that I had already started my self-development before I started Phillis Wheatly grade school.

Chapter 3 — My Early Educational Journey

It was just two years after my accident that I started grade school. Let me inject that I can't recall any special events of my childhood from the accident to me starting school. Did I know my ABC's and numbers? I don't know. I was not aware at that time that I could have had a learning disability. But as I moved further in my educational process, I said to myself that I was picking up some things but not others. There was no way at that period that children with some type of learning problem could get special studying assistance.

One day at school I heard my teacher Ms. Craven tell someone she was talking to that Jerry was somewhat retarded. I went home and asked my grandmother what that meant. She told me that it was a person who had problems with learning skills. I told her that my teacher said that to someone at school. She took me to school the next day and she talked to my teacher outside. From that point forward I read more and focused on what people would tell me, what I heard in the little two room Colored school that had all eight grades inside taught by one teacher. How many students were there I do not remember. I never counted. I was more concerned with my studies and proving to others that I was not retarded. As time passed and I moved through the educational system my learning skills were different, so I adapted and moved on. I will mention other times I felt that it was hard for me to do certain skills, that my cognitive skills were not up to the level with the other students. Remember I had survival skills that others may not have. But most of all as I learned how to write and spell, I was able to show my grandparents how to write their names. Later, I was given legal permission to sign their names along with my name.

From the first three years of school it was just two of us in the same grade, Carolyn and little Jerry. We remained as classmates until the end of the ninth-grade year. We sat at a little red table with red chairs. We had bookshelves on the north wall. The other students sat next to each other at desks. We could hear other subjects taught to the other students from our table. I listened and was picking up on what was discussed, and I saw those who did or didn't know the answers. If someone got into trouble, we all saw the punishment they received. They also witnessed my time as well. I was an active child in so many ways. I loved to talk at the wrong time, but I also talked when I was called upon by the teacher.

During recess, the bigger students play with each other and Carolyn and I would play by ourselves. That was ok. We had our own toy cars, jumping rope, and later a game for rainy days. We would swing on the south side swings for us small kids.

We had no running water inside of the school or inside restrooms. We had a common bucket of water with our cups to drink from. A trip to the separated outhouses was a journey itself. Our school had no central air, just fresh air mixed with coal dust from the nearby mines and from coal stoves in our homes that came through the six windows that were wide open. The classroom had a big coal stove in the middle of the room for heat in the winter. The older boys would keep the stove hot during that time of the year. We would go home for lunch for one hour. The school let out around 3:30 P.M. Ms. Craven and Mr. Craven lived in Fort Smith.

Our schoolbooks in many cases came from the White grade school. Many times, there were pages missing. You see the town might have been diverse, but our educational system was segregated. We did go to the White grade school for programs and plays. I don't recall them coming to our school at any time. I was so happy when I was in the second or third grades when the County Library located in Greenwood would send its Mobile Library Truck to our school. This little white lady and her driver would pull up to the school and our teacher would let us by grade go to the truck. Miss Ingram would help us select any book for our grade level. I can't remember any book titles or what I selected, but many of the students made the point that the books challenged what we were learning in school. From my personal viewpoint school itself was a challenge, the book only enforced it more. I did not think that I would become a writer later in my life. Phillis Wheatley may not be a top-level Colored school of the time, but we all learned how to survive and look out for each other and to be supportive in the years ahead. The relationships formed between all of us became stronger each day. We all developed strong values, morals, and belief systems unquestionable by any standards.

It was a basic understanding that at the end of the eight grade all the Black children had to be bussed to Fort Smith for high school. A practice for many years. The White Huntington Mansfield School District would rather pay our expenses and money to the Fort Smith School District to keep us out of White High School in Mansfield, Arkansas. I think that our Black parents felt that we were safer to be bussed thirty-five miles away than to attend the school in Mansfield.

Around 1957 or 1958, all the Black children were bussed to both Colored grade school and high school in Fort Smith. I was very unnerved when I arrived at Howard Grade School in Fort Smith. We were only there for a few months, and I was transferred to Washington Grade School in the Midland Heights area of Fort Smith. I did not know that for the next four or so years my education experience would be HELL. The Black students were very hateful and mean to us on many occasions. They threaten us by starting fights and other actions that I will not try to tell you about. That attitude was not a helpful situation for me and the other students from Huntington. How could we focus on our learning when we always had to look out for our safety.

During this time, I was hit with another change in my life. The financial situation of my grandparents became rough. We had to get Welfare food and several people in the community gave my grandfather money and he would do odd jobs.

For us to stay in our home in Huntington we had to move to the Kansas City area so that my grandfather could find work. My Grandmother knew that it would not be permanent. I felt that this would be the end of my life in Huntington.

I had to live with my Mommy, stepfather , sisters, and brothers. I adjusted well to the living condition my Mommy had. But I was given permission to go to my Aunt Doris's house each weekend where my grandparents were living. You see nine of their ten children lived in the Kansas City Area. They had support and my grandfather had a job that paid a salary so he could save enough money so we could go back to Huntington sooner.

This situation gave me the opportunity to bond with Mommy and my family. I went to a big city grade school and a large church as well. I just went with the flow and dealt with it. No outstanding events or situations occurred at this time. The only thing that influenced me was the cold weather. I would do anything in class to get out of recess. The principal would see me in the hall so much and he would ask me "what have you done now?" He approached me one day and said, "Jerry, you are doing this to stay inside during recess because of the cold weather." He was right. So, I stayed in the Principal Office until the weather got warmer.

My grandfather went back to Huntington to check on the house. While there his sister Ida died. He called my grandmother and told her. So, when we packed to return for the funeral my grandmother told me that we would not return to Kansas City after the funeral. I was so happy and I started to get my things together. We made it back. I also returned to the same grade school and same situation. But that was better than staying in Kansas City.

My connection with Mommy and my sisters and brothers continued after we returned to Huntington. Our Christmas vacations and Labor Day Weekends were visits to Kansas City on the Kansas City Southern Railway from Sallisaw, Oklahoma to Kansas City, Missouri. These train experiences only added to my life experiences. The time period when these visits happened ran from the 1960s to the 1970s.

We would leave Huntington by the mail bus or the Greyhound bus early in the morning. When we got to Fort Smith, we went to the old Union Station to take the Kansas City Southern Bus to the KCS Station in Sallisaw, Oklahoma. The train from New Orleans would arrive around 1:30 P.M. We waited for the train in the Black waiting room. Before long I could hear the train whistle in the distance, and it was about time to get on the train and around 7:45 P.M. the train would stop at Kansas City, Missouri Union Station. But what happened on that train could be a scene in a movie. Here is this one scene on the train that I remember so well.

I loved the train trips for the train was a place that kept my mind busy. I would try in many ways to explore the train and talk to the conductor and ask many questions along the way except what my correct age was when he thought my grandparents should pay half-fare for me. I would tell him that I was big for my age.

You must remember that it was still the Jim Crow era, therefore the dinner car was off limits to us. Later the Black staff from the dinner car would come through our car and sell sandwiches and drinks to us. I can say that the sandwiches were good. That also meant that we could not go to the White car for sure.

However, on one of my Christmastime trips to Kansas City I tested that policy. My Grandparents would have to sleep sometime on the trip. Well, that time came, and I went to the White car, because I knew that the White people loved to hear us Black people singing. I got through the dinner car without anyone stopping me. In the white car as passengers were Mr. and Mrs. Varner that worked in our County Court House in Greenwood, Arkansas where we paid our taxes and got our driver license. I knew then that each Christmas they would be going to see their son and his family. I just went to see them, and I sang for them as a gift for Christmas, but all the other passengers could hear me. By the way, my grandmother came after me. Before she stopped my concert, I had made some money. I did not tell her how much. Upon her arrival my grandmother applied with her hand or belt some behavior modification on the right part of my backside. That was all right because I had made money. I believed in capitalism at an early age.

This event on the train came back to bite me a few years later. Let me tell you about what happened. It was around 1982, I think, when Governor Bill Clinton was running again for the Governorship of Arkansas. He made a campaign stop in Fort Smith. In the lobby of this event we're Mr. and Mrs. Varner and me. Governor Clinton greeted them and then me. We made little talk, but the Mrs. Varner told him that my grandfather was very good friends with them, and they knew me all my life. She selected to tell the Governor about our trip to Kansas City at Christmas time. She told the Governor about my singing concert and what my grandmother did to me when she caught me singing in the White Car off limit areas for Blacks during that period in America.

The Governor enjoyed that little story, and I am sure that I turned a fare shade of red.

At the next State Convention of the Arkansas Democratic Party in Little Rock, Mr. Clinton ask me to sing the National Anthem. Mr. Clinton thanked me for the song and by surprise he retold that story that Mrs. Varner shared with him on that stop in Fort Smith. On one of his trips in the State with a State Trooper, they went through Huntington, Mr. Clinton said to the Trooper that he had a good friend from Huntington. The Trooper called out the name of Jerry Moore. Yes, that was the friend. The Troop told him that I was a dear friend of his as well. We are still friends to this day Mr. Clinton and the State Trooper. On my fiftieth Birthday I dedicated my personal papers to the University of Arkansas, Fayetteville; I was honored by that trooper with a salute. That story at the time was embarrassing to tell a Governor and later a U.S. President. The only U.S. President that I think knew about the behavior modification that I received on that train.

Chapter 4 — Bus One

Reflecting upon the days that I attended Mansfield High School is like listening to soft music. I can feel being back in time but a part of the present. My world was limited to Huntington, Arkansas, Highway 71 South to Mansfield, my family, my friends, and my church. All these things influenced what was ahead for me. Today I see this area as "Going Home," a place where I once lived. But simultaneously it was a place that has so many memories both good and bad. I can't help but think of those who have gone to the promised land.

As you read this chapter, I would like for you understand that this is my own personal account and perhaps not the account of the other Black students that entered the Mansfield School District. They have had the opportunity to write their own reflections. One fact I can share is that we loved each other and bonded together to get through the experience.

I was very surprised when I was told that the Black students would be going to Mansfield and not to Fort Smith to school at the beginning of the Fall Term of 1962. This was something that had not been expressed to us until the end of the 1961 school term. It was hard to accept because for so many years we attended school in Fort Smith after the eighth grade, but all grade levels were around 1958. I guess after seeing the racial tension each night on television, and seeing what had happened in Little Rock, mixed emotions were the norm. But you will see that we managed to escape the calling out of the National Guard, the rioting, the burning of buildings, scenes most common during this violent period. Were we able to escape these occurrences because the two races had a long history of peaceful racial relations? Or was it because the two sides did the necessary homework to avoid trouble?

To answer the first question is not hard at all. From the early days in which Huntington and Mansfield came into existence the two races were represented. They both lived and worked together in this coal mining area. If a problem arose between both groups, they worked together to find a peaceful solution. Perhaps the stage was set back early as 1887, to create an atmosphere of cooperation.

The next question, the integration process, took about three years to get all parties involved to agree on the right time to do it. According to Mr. Jack Efurd, Superintendent at that time, he had to get it through the School Board. It was not that they were against integration, but they were afraid of integrating (Efurd Interview, 1985). By integrating the schools, the district would save more money, because the district had to pay all the expenses for the Black students going to Fort Smith. A cost-effective decision and maybe the right thing to do.

According to Mr. Efurd in the interview he stated that, "a series of meetings had been held in 1961. The process to be used was outlined for the staff and faculty. Each teacher was assigned to a group to discuss the way it was to be done. Also, the process was discussed among the Blacks as a whole outlining for them the way integration would happen." (Interview 1985).

Beginning in early 1962, parents were consulted. These meetings were at first separate, then both groups came together. It was made very clear to all the parents that all students would be treated equally. Of course not everyone felt comfortable about integration. Opposition came from both sides. But as time went on the reasons for integration became clearer. The time had arrived for Bus Number One to start its engine.

Some of the other details to be worked out were to write to the surrounding districts and let them know that the Mansfield District was to integrate in the Fall of

1962. His action would give those districts time to decide how they would or wouldn't respond to the Black students who would be coming to their campuses to play sports or to compete in academic events hosted by their schools. So, you can see all the precautions which were taken to keep racial tension down in the surrounding areas of Sundown Towns.

As opening day approached, the final touches were made by all parties involved. School policies were reviewed so they could be implemented to the letter. All parties were given a final briefing. Details had not been written on the pages of history, and only those who participated in that long process had the opportunity to experience the feelings and expectations yet to come. At that point Bus Number One was ready to move out of the bus garage.

Join me as I share with you what I did the night before I got on Bus One the next morning and my first day of school. Believe it or not, that night was no different than the other nights before the start of school. I was excited and very nervous. But what might make this night different was that I would be going to Mansfield and not Fort Smith as it was in the past. I was getting ready to face another challenge in my life.

It seems like the sun came up very early that Monday morning. I got up and got dressed for the day and finished my breakfast. I looked out of the window and in the distance, I saw Bus One coming across the bridge. I had about ten minutes to go to the bus stop. So within ten minutes I would see new White people that I did know and if they would like us Blacks. The Whites that lived in Huntington on that bus were friends of ours and we interacted with them and their families for years.

At each bus stop a Black parent was standing there given us (twelve Black Students) a feeling of security. Many were at the same stop when we arrived that evening after school.

As the bus stopped and the door opened, I saw this man with a smile on his face. That smile made me feel welcome. I took my seat next to a student. I don't remember if it was as White or Black students. The ride to the school was full of excitement, as I recall. For the next six years I rode the same bus that stopped for me on that September morning. Each day was unlike the one before, for each day had its own beginning and ending. Those days on Bus One developed character in each of us.

We finally arrived at the school. As we were unloading the bus many of the students came up to us and welcomed us to the school. After about ten to fifteen minutes of talking, the bell rang. I moved with the flow as I made my way toward the auditorium. At that point I got my first glance of the teachers. I was glad to see Mr. Efurd that we all knew from the group meeting. He was standing with a smile on his face. We went to our seats in the auditorium.

The talking soon turned into quietness as Mr. Efurd made his way to the front walking heavily with his loud sounding wingtip shoes that became a strong signal or sound of authority for many auditorium events in the years he was still there. I guess it was two or three years later that he left and went to the Gentry, Arkansas School District. In later years I began to see that this man put his job and maybe his life on the line for what he and the School Board did when they integrated the school. He had a long struggle, I'm sure. He lived up to what he told us during those meetings when this day arrived. He told us that we would be treated equally and most of the time we were. I will discuss later in the chapter when I experienced intentional acts of discrimination.

The assembly lasted for about thirty minutes. Each class was dismissed to go to various classrooms to conduct first day business. At this point it was the first that Black students were separated since arriving at the school.

Reality hit me at that time. I had the opportunity to meet and see my other classmates. I felt lucky because many of my classmates lived in Huntington as well as the teacher. After about thirty minutes we had the opportunity to run through our schedule. Each class set rules, got our textbook, locker numbers, and were given our assigned seats in each class.

Our first day of class ended around one P.M. Bus Number One was ready to return me back home where I talked for hours with my Grandparents about the daily activities and my personal reactions. That day went without any trouble. That first week for me was learning about everything. I began to interact with my classmates. Building lasting relationships and soon finding out which classmate(s) would be a challenge for me. My love for school got better. Also, I was a little older and felt that I understood myself more and could make decisions on my own with some influence from someone else if I needed.

The second week of school was still new but moving my first week into history. I believe it was during that second week or soon later it was time to elect Class Officers and Student Council Representatives. Our class got the Class Officer out of the way. I just voted because I did not know those who were nominated. The time came for the two Student Council nominees. Out of the blue I heard my name. What is going on, I said to myself. Someone was playing a joke. A blonde headed white boy called my name. I asked him his name after the election and why did he call my name? He told me that his name was Dewayne Hope. After he nominated me, another guy said, "I call for the vote." No one else was nominated and I won. The first Black student on the Student Council. He told me he knew I could do the job. I felt it was his efforts that were to later backfire on him.

From that day forward Dewayne and his little friends did their best to make jokes they thought about me or ask me something stupid, but they were showing me their IQ level and not making racial statements. I told myself that I would watch them and learn more about them and why they thought like that or was the only way I would know more about me and how I was thinking as a Black person. I stayed on the student council for years. Dewayne did not understand that I took my experience on the Student Council and other clubs later that it would lead to my present-day political involvement that has opened doors for me in the local, state and national political arenas. What could have been racial harassment helped me to build my self-esteem and be at many decision-making tables in my future. In today's terms, these boys would be called Rednecks. By observing their acts in the years ahead gave me a strong foundation on how to deal with the white race and status-based individuals I have had the opportunity to interact with as well. I was able to gain the support of my class and classmates in many ways. I will always be grateful for that election.

But by ninth-grade things began to change a little when it came to my interactions, mainly with teachers. This first story was racial as viewed by others, but I enjoyed it because I won this little situation with my basketball coach who was also my math teacher. I told you in another chapter about my trip to Kansas City during the Christmas break. On my trip around the ninth-grade and tenth-grade years I was given permission to do basketball practice with my brother's high school team.

Coach Ross always had games during The Holiday Classic for Kansas City High Schools. This got me out of my Mommy's house and from my other sisters and brothers. I also enjoyed running around with city Black guys. I could travel with the team if there were out-of-town games on my visits. I loved that opportunity to practice with them, making me a better player back home. But my Kansas City basketball practices was not noticed by my coach. I would show James and Larry and others on the second team that I sit on the bench with some of these new plays I learned in Kansas City. I had a feeling that my coach saw me, for he never missed anything that I would do while at practice. I guess he felt I was in his territory and the others that I was practicing with would listen to me. So one day after a session since it was the last period of the day, he called me to his office. He got to the point. He said, "Jerry, I have seen you trying to tell and show your little group of players some moves that was not in my play book, I think that those moves were from your brother's team in Kansas City, let me make it clear we do not play "nigger ball" and you must stop it now." My reply was "Coach Jackson if we would try some of these "nigger ball plays" we could win more of our games, Sir." He was so angry that he looked but could not say a word. I left the office with a smile on my face, what could he do to me? Put me off the team that would have been ok with me. As time moved on, I noticed at some of our games he was using similar plays and I continued to show my teammates after a trip new plays, for I know he was using them without being open to me about it. I love it.

At the end of eighth grade it was time to select classes for my ninth-grade years. It was the start of having grade points at the end of each semester that would determine our Class Ranking. My Counselor called me to his office to show me my proposed class schedule for next year. One showed that you went to high school to take a trade or business job and the other if you went to college, you would not be prepared for even Freshman level college classes. I told him that the schedule did not work for me. I made it clear that I was going to college, and I needed College Prep classes. We had a brief discussion. I made a point to tell him that I felt that I was smart enough for those classes. I ask him point blank, "you don't think I can?" I suggested that he made a new proposed schedule for me, and I would come back. When I came back, he showed me what we put together for me, and I accepted it and went on my way. I did state that if I didn't make a three-point GPA at the end of my ninth-grade year he could change it, my College Prep classes were never changed for the following years. I graduated number twelve out of sixty-four in the class that graduated. The grade point I had at the end of my ninth-grade year helped me to be the first Black student in the school history to be inducted into the National Beta Club Honor Society. My membership in this club gave me the opportunity to go to state meetings in Little Rock where we had to stay in a hotel or motel overnight. From that time I would always have a private room on all trips requested by my grandparents not just for Beta Club conventions but all school related trips until I graduated from high school.

The next situation was not as simple as the others mention. It was the custom of several of our teachers to give us our points before Report Cards to know what grade we would receive. My Civic teacher Coach Tate took one day to do just that for my class. He skips me the first time around. After he completed the first round, I raised my hand and told him that he skipped me. Several in the class said that he did not give me my points. I ask him to please give me my points. He went on with class discussion. I told him that it was not fair to me. He told me in front of the whole that he would no longer put up with my smart attitude. He would bring me up in front of the class for punishment and going against him, and that he would pull my pants down so the class could see my smart black ass. Some of the students laughed. I was so outdone that I put my things together and went to the office to report to the principal.

I waited in the Principal's Office because he was teaching the other Civic class at that time. As soon as the principal returned to the office, I told him that I needed to talk to him and the superintendent. When we arrived at the Superintendent Office, I told them both what Coach Tate said to me in front of the class. They ask me what they should do. I gave two choices — (1) not to renew his contract and (2) I would tell my grandfather. I gave them two weeks to solve the situation. If not resolved by that time my grandfather would bring me to school to have a meeting with the three of them. Within two weeks his contract was not renewal, and I never told my grandfather about the situation. I was transferred to the other Civic class the next day. I stood up to this teacher because if he could get by doing it to me other students could be the next victim.

The following situation would enforce my thoughts that I had strong support of many of my classmates. Our high school had a final exam policy that if you had perfect attendance or an excuse absent in a class with an B average you would not have to take the Final Exam. In April of 1968 Dr. Martin Luther King Jr. was killed. The Black families in Huntington ask the school to excuse us to see Dr. King's service on television. One of my teachers did not accept my excuse to be absent for that day. The teacher read the list for those exempted from the Final Exam under the policy my name was not on the list. When I reminded the teacher, they did not see his services as an excuse to be absent since I was not one of his relatives. I ask if the office had given them the note about us having an excuse to be absent on that day? It was stated that I would take the Final Exam. One student stepped up and said that they would take it if I had to take it, and before long several of the students who were exempted said that they would take their exam. As a result I did not have to take the exam. That is one example that I had support from some of my classmates.

As I walked at my graduation on May 14, 1968, with my class, I felt ready and prepared to move on to college. With the support and fairness of many of my teachers and others at Mansfield High School those six years helped me in the development of my values, morals, belief system, spirituality, self-esteem and the assurance I knew who I was without second guessing.

As I transitioned into the next phase of my journey, my name was changed from Jerry Harris Jr. to Jerry Harris Moore. It was through the adoption process by my grandparents that I was able to get financials assistance through their Social Security benefits to attend college, as well as a good financial graduation gift from Mr. B.A. McConnell, a friend of my grandfather to be used for my college tuition.

Chapter 5 — Beacon of Hope

When I finished high school, I did not sit down and write a five- or ten-year plan of action. It was not clear what was ahead of me other than that I would go to college. At the end of a four-year period of college I would get a job teaching high school. I thought of coming back to Mansfield to start my career. I must enroll and pass my classes and get a degree before I could apply for that job. I felt that I was going to achieve that goal. Hard work and staying focused would be my challenge.

At the same time, I thought how I should begin to support my grandparents. They were getting older, and their health had begun to decline. So, I said to myself, I must work and go to college at the same time, for that to happen. I recalled the hard time we had just a few years ago. My grandfather and I would do odd jobs in Huntington and would sometimes go to Waldron, Arkansas to help a friend of his that he had known for years. I also worked at the grocery store each Wednesday cleaning floors and cleaning the doctor's office as well. That gave me some money to help.

I was excited at the end of May of 1968, after graduating from high school, so I could enroll at Westark Junior College in Fort Smith. It was just two weeks after high school that I became a college student. Was I ready? I would soon find out if I was ready or not. My first day of college arrived and the journey began.

I passed my first courses in college with good grades. I took off the second term of summer but was ready for the Fall Term. The Fall semester I took a full load of twelve hours of courses. Reality hit me in the face that semester. I studied hard and socialized a lot at the same time. I was truly like a typical college student. What made it a little easier was the relationships I had with my teachers. The next year with these teachers I was well prepared for my transfer to the University of Arkansas. For example, my English teacher was aware of my disability, she approached me one day and said that she would like to assist me with my grammar and sentence structure, and would I be willing to accept her help one day a week if we could meet. I said it was ok and I gave her a time that we could meet. She gave me things to read into a recorder and play it back so I would be aware of how it all sounded as I spoke. Then she had me to write something that would show me what was wrong with my writing, especially verb tense. She did this for me on her days off, I later learned.

In another situation, my education teacher was working on her dissertation at the University of Mississippi dealing with classroom experience. She developed a program for those of us going into education, a partnership with some of the elementary and junior high schools in Fort Smith and Van Buren as teacher assistants with a teacher at those schools. This was to prepare us for our classroom experience later. During this program, I was assigned to an elementary school in Van Buren and a junior high school in Fort Smith. I was interviewed by the local newspaper as well about that early classroom experience.

I mentioned that I would sooner or later get a job to help with expenses. Many of my high school classmates were working at the Dr. Pepper Bottling Plant in Fort Smith. So I went to apply for a part-time job. I got a job as a truck loader for the next day. I had worked for the pop truck drivers at Hunter's Store in Huntington sorting out pop bottles for each of the companies, about four or five companies. I got from fifty cents to one dollar from each company per trip and averaged two trips a week. When the drivers did not pay me on time their bottles were not sorted. If they agreed to pay for the present load, I would make them pay for two weeks in advance. It would cost them one dollar per trip if they paid fifty cents; after that those paying one dollar per trip would go up to two dollars per trip.

Two weeks before the Final Exams at Westark I asked the co-owner of the plant for two days off to study for my finals. She said no, and I could adjust my schedule during the day before work and after work. I did not make a big deal out of the decision. The next day at work I gave my two-week notice. You see, passing my exams was more important than that low paying job, but I had faith that a better job would come my way very soon. Three years later I had the opportunity to thank her for encouraging me to make a decision that was best for me. At a Parent Night at Northside High School, she walked into her daughter's class, and I was the teacher. Surprise! I greeted all the Parents, but I asked her to stand, and I said, "If it wasn't for you, I would have stayed at my job at your plant taking the risk of failing my exams, but today I am your daughter's teacher. Because of your guidance I made the right choice."

I did not wait too long before I saw a job opening at a local nursing home, Spark's Manor, for a weekend Orderly for the 3:00–11:00 P.M. position. I told my grandparents about that job. They both said to take it because they saw that it would benefit them in the years ahead. This working experience was one of the best jobs I ever did. I thought taking care of these elderly people would be depressing, but it was not, I gained positive feelings each day that made things easy therefore I did continue my education at Westark Community College and on to the University of Arkansas.

The administration and staff were very supportive. We worked great together. I missed very few weekends. I also assisted the nurses and the female staff with their residents in lifting and roll over their attendees in bed. I would sometimes help to feed them as well. That way, no one was overworked. Even the Head Nurse would assist me in making the beds. That way they could see if I was doing it correctly.

I had residents that were from all positions in society with various backgrounds and experiences. When I was in their room assisting them, they would share with me their life story. I learned more about real history and true-life experiences than I had or will read in my classes at the college. Each conversation would be good term paper material in my history class. One resident experienced the Holocaust I believe, for we had another male staff member that could not go into his room, because each time he would speak loudly the name "Hitler" and the staff member would have to find me to calm him down. So we switched residents.

When I was studying World War I, one my residents had been an International Correspondent for an American Publication stationed in Paris, France. I asked him what it was like in Paris. He shared with me one of his assignments after the war and during the Peace Talks and the forming of the League of Nations. One assignment he talked about was covering President Woodrow Wilson's trip to the Peace Conference. One day as he was leaving his hotel to cover the President he was going through the revolving door, the person on the other side came through and hit him, causing the paperwork in his hand to fall to the floor. The other person was General John J. Pershing, the U.S. Commander.

As I recall, the Vietnam War was going on at this time. Again, I came closer to the war without being there. Each afternoon when I worked in another wing of the Nursing Home, I had a resident who would get a call from a friend each week and another person each day around the same time. It seemed that each call would come when my resident was in the restroom, therefore, I had to answer it and tell him who was calling. Well, the once-a-week caller was an older person, and he would give me his first name of Omar. Several weeks later my resident, Dr. McNamara, said that the general was late with his call. The only person calling at that time was Omar. The call came and I quickly said, hello General. Omar made it clear that was never to address him as General, but always Omar. The only General I knew that had a first name of Omar was the Four-Star General Omar Bradley. That was him. I continued to address him as Omar until I moved on.

The other call came from a cousin of his named Bobby. I would leave the room when I was finished with my job in his room. Again, this person was late in calling and Dr. McNamara said I guess the Secretary is busy. It was his cousin the Secretary of Defense under President Johnson. When I addressed him by his official title, he told me that I could not use that position from that day forward, so it was always Bobby from that time forward.

At home one night during the evening news my grandparents and I were watching the news and the anchor person said the man standing in the window of this building in D.C was Secretary McNamara. I told my Grandparent that I talked to this person each afternoon when he called his cousin at the Nursing Home.

One of the other things I learned by working at the nursing home was the importance of having children. I saw firsthand the role my resident's children played in their parent's life at this stage of their life. Many were very good to them and visited on a regular basis. But I had those who would only visit twice a year in some cases, for whatever reason. Many were very lonely, and relatives only visited to be kept in the Will. I saw many Christmases, birthdays, Mother's and Father's Days when no children came to visit many of the residents. Many told me that their family would not come because they were too busy. Many had not seen family since they were put in that place. Some lived out of town and state, some lived across town. The only gift if they got one would be a box of chocolate covered cherries that they can't have, or a Christmas plant.

What hit me at that time was, would I have children? Not knowing my Dad I was cautious in rushing out and having kids. I was afraid that I would have kids that would not be there for me when I got to that stage. Also, what if I had a kid or kids and the mother would not be with me and not tell them about me. We'd divorce and she'd take the kid(s) and leave me and put me out to pasture. I thought hard about this. But it was not until later that I made the decision to stay single because this could happen to me just like I saw what happened to some of the residents at the Nursing Home.

I came back and worked at the Nursing Home during Christmas break, the first summer at the University of Arkansas, and at the end of that summer. The administration and staff gave me a surprise Going Away Party, presenting me with a watch. Also at that time, I had a big Student National Education Convention in San Francisco. They give me a two weeks' paycheck to help me out. I did drop by when I was at home for a visit for some time after I had left. Since the time I worked at Spark's Manor, advancement in what we call Assistance Living has changed. More legal standards have been put into place on how these centers are operated and better treatment of its residents has been enforced. With all these legal standards in place, I would like to stay in my home longer with Home Health Care Services that are covered by the Affordable Health Care Act. Surely, I can find somebody willing to stay with me at that time in my life.

At the end of my time working at Spark's Manor and finishing my degree at Westark, I became involved in the Arkansas Student Education Association. This association assists those of us majoring in education with certain issues related by providing more training and awareness of what improvement is needed to prepare us for our future time in the classroom. At the end of the Spring Semester 1970, Westark Student Club nominated me to run for State Vice President of Student Arkansas Education Association. I was elected, making me the First Black officer in the history of the State Association.

We went to the Southeastern Regional Convention of Student National Education Association in New Orleans later in the summer and I was elected as Regional Director, a position like the President of the group. I think we had about eight or nine States in our Region. I served for one year. After, that year Arkansas was moved to the Central Regional with Missouri, Kansas, Texas, Louisiana, Oklahoma and New Mexico. I was elected as the Regional Director. It was my duty to promote the educational goals of the region as well as being its representative to the Student National Education Association Convention each year.

For those two years my traveling schedule was arranged around by college classes. I was given travel time from Thursday to Monday when I had meetings out of state. Upon my return to campus, I would schedule a meeting with the University Student Education Organization officers and the sponsor to update them on the most recent legislation dealing with education. Also, I scheduled a meeting with the Dean of the College of Education of the University and the University's President to keep them informed of what I was doing while Representing the University. Each time I returned to campus I had to get back to my studies and classes. I did not miss class because the time I had to miss was enough. I failed my first class ever in school. The teacher stated that I missed too many classes, it seems that he would schedule each test on a day I had a meeting scheduled out of town. He would not let me take the test before I left but told me that I had to take a make-up test. When I saw my failing grade at the end of the semester I called and scheduled a meeting with him.

It did not go well, he did not change my grade. I later found out that all the Black Basketball players in the class passed the class even though they missed classes for games and a week for tournaments. I had to take the class over and got a B with a different teacher.

During this time I was asked to represent the Student National Education Association at the White House Conference on Children and Youth in Education. I can recall the first time I saw the Lincoln Memorial at 3:00 A.M. in the morning and in front of The Lincoln Memorial I called the Arkansas Hogs. The next evening I had dinner at the White House hosted by President Richard M. Nixon. The person next to me at my table was the education minister from France.

I did the sightseeing tour of the Capitol Building, and Arlington Cemetery. Each place was so emotional for me. As I looked up at President Lincoln I began to cry. Here I am standing where my grandparents, who were uneducated, never had the opportunity to see but their baby was standing there. I couldn't wait to share this experience with them when I got home.

I returned home on Saturday after being at the White House two days before. I returned to reality. I had to focus on what was going on at home and the welfare of grandparents before I left for the University. I remember so well that after church that Sunday afternoon my Grandparents ask me to go with them to the dump to collect glass bottles to wash and break up so I could take them to the Glass Plant before leaving for the University and sell the glass, so they could get food and have some money before I received my expense check from my trip to D.C. The next weekend when I came home, I had money to help with the bills.

Our national and regional meetings had some strong debates and hot discussions of what was viewed by some as options on issues and ideas confronting education in the United States. Radical student organizations came to our meetings, making the situation unsafe at times. This division was centered around liberal and radical viewpoint dealing the American Educational Policies. At this time one radical group of students were trying to put into the office some of their people. Therefore, the National Election Committee was put under protection to make sure that the election would be fair. Only members of the election committee could room with each other with our rooms assigned in a different wing of the hotel from other members with unlisted room numbers at the front desk. Yes, I was on that committee too. I had the same roommate at each meeting, and we are still close friends today.

This brings up another topic and this is a great place to discuss it. I have made many friends over those years. It was at this time I began to think about marriage. I met some wonderful young ladies from across this country. Some of these ladies talked about building a relationship that could lead to marriage. Being a typical male, I gave it some thought. I went in a direction that felt was safe for all of us. Let's be friends for a while and get to know each other. It was not as easy to get along with me as it may seem. If a strong relationship was built, if it did not work out in the courting stage, it would not cause bad feelings or total hate for each other in the end. For when you reach intimacy it is another story, it may lead to children causing more risk in the relationship. I did not want to feel like I had been in that turnabout I struggled with in D.C. So, for the years to follow I did my best to stay focused on what were to be my purposes in life.

My work in the Student National Education Association gave me the opportunity to work through a situation slowly and not rush because it may not turn out for the best. My experience and leadership skills also were a strong point when I was chosen to be the second Black teacher at Northside High School in 1972. I have always thought of myself as an open-minded person and a good listener as well.

I enjoyed my college years. I became a typical college student in many ways. Going to the university, I lived with people I did not know in the dorm. The dining hall was a combination of all people from around the world. My Resident Assistance in the dorm from time to time were either white or black. My friends that I got to build relationships with were of both races as well. What a great experience during those years. Since I was from Huntington this diversity was not hard for me to adjust to. My first semester in the dorm my roommate was a classmate of mine from Westark. His parents came for a visit and saw that we were roommates. They had him to move out that day. I was at home that weekend and when I returned all his things were out of the room. I saw him in the hall, and he told me that his parents told him that he could not room with a Black person. I said OKAY, and that was fine with me. What I really enjoyed was that I would have a private room at no extra cost.

As a result of my D.C. trip to the White House Conference on Children and Youth, The Dean of the College of Education at the university called me to come by his office as soon as I could. When I arrived for the meeting the Dean told me that the Governor's Office called him to submit one of their students to work with his office as they plan the Arkansas White House Conference on Children and Youth 1970. The Dean told me that he had nominated me for that position. I was speechless for about two minutes. I said OKAY and rushed back to my room to call my grandparents and tell them. This would require me to go to meetings in Little Rock. Before that first meeting the Governor's Office called me and told me that Governor Rockefeller would like me to chair one of the committees for the conference on Elementary and Secondary Education in Arkansas.

The day for the Planning Committee to meet was scheduled at the Capitol. I went to Huntington before the meeting and left there to go to Little Rock. I arrived at the Governor's Office and was taken to his Office at once. I walked in and there stood that tall man. We greeted each other. He asked if I had let my grandparents know that I had arrived in Little Rock. I said not yet. He handed me his gold-plated telephone for me to ask the operator to connect me with my home phone in Huntington. I could hear my grandmother on the phone, and I said hello, Mother. I made it to Little Rock just fine. I would call back when I started back to Huntington. At that point in time the Governor asked to speak to her. I handed him the phone, and he talked to her and then my Grandfather briefly. I was so happy that they had the opportunity to talk to a Governor who was a Rockefeller.

Several meetings followed that one. On many occasions I had to go for a meeting and sometime dinner at the Governor's private home on Petit Jean Mountain near Morrilton, Arkansas. Those meetings and dinners there set the stage for me again for years to come. I to this day say, "If you can have dinner with a Rockefeller what would top that off during your lifetime?" I put that experience above the White House Dinner for a personal reason. I stayed in connection with him during his re-election campaign and after through his son Paul Winthrop. During his campaign I worked to have one of his campaign stops in Fort Smith at Quinn Chapel AME Church in the Black community. Paul Win was in Fayetteville campaigning for Lt. Governor the day I was celebrating my fiftieth Birthday at a Luncheon held at the Old Post Office, and he joined our group, and I told those attending about how we met at his Father's home when I was there for meetings and dinner. He went on to win his election.

I guess it was in the Spring of 1972 on one of my week-end trips home that another situation happened that made Arkansas History in one way or another. It was a Saturday morning that my grandmother and I were shopping in Mansfield, Arkansas about two miles south of Huntington when we came out of the drug store going to the car that I looked down the sidewalk and saw Bill Clinton campaigning for Congress against John Paul Hammerschmidt, the present representative. I introduced Bill to my grandmother. I told her that this was my friend from the University. I mentioned that he taught in the Law School and that we would have lunch one to two times a week in the Student Union. They talked as he walked her to the car, and he opened the door for her and helped her into the car. I told him that I would see him later in the week. We started back home my grandmother looked over to me and said, "Continue your friendship with that young man for some day he will be the President of America." She was right. The next week while at lunch I told Bill what she said to me, and he said sure!!! Like that will ever happen.

He held State offices before he became President. I worked in all his campaigns and elections from that time forward. Upon his election as President Elect, I wrote a private letter reminding him again what my grandmother said about him becoming President. Later his team called me and offered me a position in his Administration, and I said No. I felt that it would be to my best interest to stay away from D.C. Also, I was thinking about what would happen if I could not do the job and that would hurt the friendship that I had with him. I have this firm belief that once you are friends you remain that in thought and mind forever, even though you do not have the regular or personal connection that you once had. But I know for sure that he will remember me if we run into each other again. I still tell people that I am a friend of Bill Clinton.

Back to the University after that encounter with Bill Clinton I brought the chapter to a conclusion in the best way possible. You see it was in my final semester before graduation that the previous discussion happened. I was enrolled in classes that would prepare me for student teaching called "Block Classes." I would request a secondary school in Fort Smith as my Student Teaching assignment so I could be at home with no rent or other expenses. Again, I would have dealt with a situation I knew was racial in many ways. One of my classes in the block was Technique of Teaching. I cannot recall what the context of the class was. Like most classes the student and teacher would engage in an exchange of ideas and thoughts. The students would raise their hands up to be called on by the teacher. One day, I have a question and after several attempts to get the teacher to see my hand raised, he would continue to talk, but if a White student raised their hand, he will respond. I would again raise my hand and he was still not responding, I told him that I had my hand up and he could see it since it was black. He went on talking. I collected my material and left the classroom. I am sure he was glad that I left. But what came later hit him in the face and in front of the entire class. The classroom door opens and there stood the Dean of the College of Education who told him to report to his office NOW!!

I returned to the next class so I could get a grade. I did not say a word for the rest of the classes. I got a C for the class. That was not the end of the story. My second semester at Northside, the high school would have a site review by the Accreditation Group for Secondary School called North Central. Each teacher was given a week for the site visit, so we did not schedule tests. On that day the class would be a lecture with student participation on that day with a textbook and discussion outline for the person who would be in the classroom. I don't recall if we were given their names. The day arrived and everything was ready. Dr. Gary Taylor came to one of my classes. I introduced Dr. Taylor to the class and related to them the day that he refused to answer my question. I told them that I felt it was for racial reasons.

After the introduction, two of my male students went to each in front of the class. Another student spoke up and told him that he was unfair because I was the most trusted teacher that they had at the school. So the class made the decision for me, forcing him to leave the classroom and the class discussion began once he left and the doors were closed.

But before this happened, I had to do Student Teaching. I was assigned to Kimmons Junior High School in Fort Smith. I was placed in the ninth-grade Civics course, with the head teacher being Mr. Owen Davis. After a week of observation, I was given the class by myself. I had to start putting together my Lesson Plan and outline my discussion. My first topic was the Soviet Union. Guess what? I had Russian History while in college, so I had knowledge of the subject. The class went very well. My students were great and very respectable toward me. I had no problems at any time. Therefore, it was a very good experience for me, and I felt ready to take on a full-time teaching job when it was offered to me.

Near the end of the semester Mr. Farnsworth, Principal of Northside High School came to the school for an assembly with all ninth graders about Northside. I was in the room and Mr. McDaniels, Principal of Kimmons, introduced me to him. One day Mr. McDaniels asked if I grew up in Fort Smith. I said no that I grew up in Huntington. He said that at one time he was Principal at Huntington Grade School, and it was in the 1950s. He related to me that one day while there a young Black kid was in a bad car accident in front of the Huntington Post Office. He asked me if I knew the person. I said yes and it was me. He was surprised that it was me.

A few weeks after the assembly Mr. McDaniels came to my classroom and told me that Mr. Farnsworth would like to meet with me after school if I could and I said yes.

I arrived soon after school was out, I met him in his office at Northside. We had a good discussion. Would I be offered a job at that big school? That night our dinner conversation was an update of that meeting. I told my grandparents that I couldn't believe it, me teaching at Northside.

Later in the week I was informed that the Duty Superintendent for the Fort Smith Special School District was at his office. We had a two-hour meeting. At the end of the meeting, he offered me a job in the district and assign me to Northside to teach Negro History, Arkansas History and any other social studies class available. Yes, I had my first teaching job before I completed my Student Teaching. Upon my return to the University, I wasted no time telling my Teachers and classmates that I had my job already. Someone had the nerve to tell me that I was hired to meet Affirmative Action Law requirement for the district because I was Black. I did not think it was fair to say that to me at that time.

I was one hour short to meet my graduation requirements. I returned to the university for the first semester of summer and took Far East History and General Sociology to meet the requirement. I called Mr. Farnsworth to ask if I could add High School General Sociology and he said yes. Therefore, I introduced Sociology for the first time in the list of classes at Northside. It was not hard for me to switch from History to Sociology for my Masters.

Chapter 6 — New Challenges Ahead

This chapter will cover three major areas of my life at the same time—First, coming to Northside High School, my first job in education. Second, the death of my grandparents very soon in my teaching career. Finally, my community involvement. Each of the areas affected me in a very mixed fashion and the handling of my interactions was a maturing and self-developmental experience. Bear with me on this part of my journey with an open mind, try not to be judgmental please?

The summer of 1972 was a busy time for me. I got a new car with the first two months payment paid for me, by the owner of the dealership in Waldron, Arkansas that knew my great, great grandfather Calvin Moore as a gift to me. I used that time preparing for my job and thinking about what was waiting for me as I walked into my first class of students and my own classroom. I read my textbooks that I would use for my courses. I made notes and lecture outlines. I practiced daily and worked on my presentation and how I would react if a student asked me a question or how to handle disciplining problems if any came up during class. I made sure that I could get into my classroom before the first day to set it up. This gave me the opportunity to take my grandparents with me. I cannot forget their expressions as they walked into my classroom. To this day I can see the smiles on their faces and tears in their eyes. I knew that it would be ok for my grandparents to bless my classroom with a spirit that was in that room each day to come. We talked all the way home about what I might need that I did not already have. Yes, that little baby that came to be with them at seventeen months is making them proud. I heard my grandmother talking on the phone to other relatives and friends about their visit to my classroom. Ms. Repass came by that evening and everything we did that day was repeated to her. She had tears in her eyes as she kissed me.

My first day had arrived and I got to school hours before the first bell would ring. I began to meet other teachers and staff members, that I did not introduce myself to at our preschool workshops. The time was near for the bell to sound, so I made sure that I was standing in the hallway at the door of my classroom to greet each student. I had on a new outfit that was in style for the 70s. I realized that what I did that day would become a standard for the next eight years. After I thought all the students were in the room I walked in and closed the door. The noise level was that of excitement for us all. I called the class to order, called the roll, followed up by introducing myself and telling a little about my background and how happy I was to have them as my first class of students in my first job as a teacher. I made it clear that they would always be my first class. I looked to my right and asked each student to give their name and tell all of us something about them.

It was time to share with them some classroom rules. Rule one was to respect each other while in class. I mention that many of our topics of discussion would not be accepted by all but let each one express what is on their mind and have constructive responses even if you disagreed. I assured them that I would be fair and treat each of them with respect. This was repeated at the start of each class that followed on that first day.

I started with the statement, "that I would not give them homework." All material would be covered in that class or the next one. I would teach from an outline that I would put on the blackboard or on the overhead project as I talked about the topic. I would give essay test questions, but each question would cover the material discussed in class or in the textbook. To be fair, there would be a review session the day before the test day. I always announced the test days in advance. My attendance on test day would be perfect on many occasions. The office noticed that some of my students would be in my class but had missed the class before or after on those test days. You see, I had students working in the Office that would observe and report to me about what they saw.

At times the students had trouble understanding what was true or was I joking with them. One day Gusto, a student said to me, "Mr. Moore it seems that you are jiving us." He would from time to time slip and call me "Mr. Jive." It was not in a disrespectful manner. Later other students would call me "Uncle J". Many to this day call me that because I was like an "Uncle" that they may or may not have had as a part of their development. Most of my classes were racially mixed so being called "Uncle J" included all the students. When I attended church, students at church would sometimes address me in front of their parents by that name. I would hear parents calling and addressing me by that name also. To this day I have former students calling me and checking on me.

Another teaching method I used was Learning Style teaching. Each student filtered information differently. You are either Audio, Visual or Kinetic (both A and V). I lectured using these methods and my test questions were written to reflect these styles as well. So I used records of present artists of popular music to explain my points and how it related to their life. I made it clear that music is a result of our interaction with others in our society, setting the stage for the world we must deal with in many ways. Let me share with you a story between Eugene and me in 1974 or 75.

One day in class as we were preparing for an upcoming test I played a song by the group, Earth, Wind and Fire, "Keep Your Head to the Sky (Phillip Bailey). Eugene would sit in the back row next to the window. As I started the lecture before long, he would close his eyes making me think that he was not into the lecture. I later found out that I was wrong because he was listening. One day in 1974 or 1975 I was on break between classes. I returned to start teaching and halfway through the lecture I saw Eugene in his old seat with his eyes closed. I said he was at his old self. After class I greeted him, and he gave me a big hug. Eugene related a situation he had in Vietnam. While in a fox hole with bullets flying over his head, he closed his eyes and, in that mood, he could hear the song, Keep Your Head to the Sky and could hear my voice speaking to him. I said nothing at this point. He continued to tell me that he made a promise if he was saved and made it back to Fort Smith, Arkansas he would find me and tell me to my face that I cared for him and all the other students because if I didn't, he would not have had that moment in Vietnam. He proved to me that with his eyes closed during class he understood what I was teaching him for he used the best learning style that worked for him which was audio. So from that point forward I did not take it for granted that if students did not engage in discussion they are not learning.

    At times you are called upon by your students to be a listener for them when they need someone outside of family and friends just to listen and give advice to them because of your trustworthiness. I was in my classroom during my planning period when I heard a knock on my door. I went and opened the door and there stood one of my Black female students with a sad look on her face. I welcomed her in and asked what was wrong. She said that she just learned that she was pregnant. She came to me because I knew her parents and she wanted help in telling them the news. We talked about what she was thinking at this point and what she wanted to do in the days ahead and after the birth. She said that at that point she only wanted to return to school after birth and finish high school. I suggested that she be open with both parents and ask for assistance so she could be a good parent like them. Do not feel that she did anything wrong. But to tell the Father to be and let him deal with the situation in his own way not what she wanted him to do. What would be best for the baby. I let her know that I would be glad to visit with her parents and what role I would play as your teacher and family friend. It worked out just fine. That baby girl today is about forty-five years old.

    The next story is about Jeff. He had a small group of followers who were also in my class. I got Jeff involved in more class discussion by calling on him when I was lecturing to get his views. I felt that other teachers did not include Jeff in their class. The other members of his group became engaged. His grades improved and he got a C the next grading period. He told me at the end of class that this was the highest grade he had made to date. What happened after that? One day I was out driving, and I needed to get gas for my car. I saw a gas station a block away. I had never stopped there before. As I pulled in this young guy came out to put gas in my car and it was Jeff. I was shocked. He spoke with a smile on his face and said hello. I told him how much gas I wanted. He started the pump. I got out of my car while he was filling it up and here walked an older man. Jeff told me that he was his father. He said to him that I was Mr. Moore/Uncle J his teacher at Northside that he got the C in on his report card. His Father said hello and that he wanted to thank me for helping Jeff, and I was the only teacher he had had while in school that took a concern in him as a person and not judged him based on his looks and dress. His Father said that I could stop at his station anytime and would get all my gas free until I left Northside.

    It may seem that I had no problems in the classroom. But I had students that would not do the work, miss classes, and were somewhat rude at times toward me. At the time some were just short of making racial comments. I learned to be as diplomatic as possible in my responses. I had one student that told me in class when I called him out for something he was doing in class replied that I was not saying anything important for him to listen to me. He was put out of class and sent to the Office. I told the counselor to move him to another teacher because it was not good for the class if he returned. I am sure I had other situations that I have forgotten. My goal was to not build a classroom of conflict and drama if possible.

What more could I do to learn more about students? I became a co-sponsored the Future Teachers of America Club, and the Black Student Association. But I really enjoyed it when I was asked to be a teacher sponsor on the student bus to a sport event out of town. I spent many Friday Nights in Little Rock and Pine Bluff at football and basketball games. This duty gave me the opportunity to build stronger relationships with the students and parents who were on the bus. The parents got to know me and saw how much I cared for the students. This knowledge became important if I had to assist a parent with conflict between them and their child as part of the job of parenting. These relationships did not always set up well with the principal because I became a threat to him, because the parents would come to me and not him for advice. I had no problems at any time. Even when no bus trip was made, I would drive the drummers to out of town games to play for the girl drill team who perform at half time. I got a speeding ticket on one trip, so we stayed overnight and came home on Saturday morning.

Each day was not always full of fun with no problems. Many times I cried with my students as well as laughing with them. If a question was asked in class, I made it a point to stop and explain before moving forward. I took textbook material and applied it to the real world so that my students could deal with real life situations. I felt that each was learning something. It became my policy that no student would receive an F grade in my classes. This policy gave my students the opportunity to have a pleasant experience.

The location of Northside made it possible to take field trips to observe real society at the little restaurant a block away from the school. The demographic setting of Northside, which included mixed racial groups, all the economic groups from low class to Old Money families was an advantage to better understand sociological theory.

I like to think that the conflict between the principal and me was my teaching methods in my classroom, but at times seem to have a racial and personal tone. My technique was beyond the traditional method of the old school. He would say to others that I was entertaining them and not helping them to learn. He would stand outside of my classroom and listen to me teaching and all he could hear was the students laughing, and that the noise level was high, so learning was not going on inside. He could conclude that I was just clowning around. But on a visit to the church that he attended he saw me inside of the sanctuary and he pushed his wife back out the door and left the building. I saw that and my mind was made up that he did not like me for whatever his reasons were. So I lost respect for him, and I could no longer stay at Northside.

At this time, I had to deal with my personal life and my job. About three weeks after starting at Northside my grandfather died. What I came to face in the months and years ahead was very hard for me. My role at home changed, for I was the Man of the House and I had to help my grandmother through our loss. My grandparents had been together for fifty-three years. It became harder as the years passed. About a year later I had to have help with my grandmother for health reasons. I soon learned that my Aunt Doris would leave her job and that she and her two children would move in with us in Huntington. I assisted in the moving by buying a car for her. I paid the expenses for my grandmother and me.

My grandmother had a stroke. Me and my aunt were working full-time so grandmother had to go to Kansas City to stay with an aunt who did not work. I went in the summer and moved her to my Mommy's house so I could help with us because the aunt she was living with did not like me and I could not and would not stay there. How I was treated when I was there for Christmas was not good. I sent money to my Mommy to help my grandmother. Some of her children did their best to get my Grandmother's Social Security check sent to Kansas City, but I had the only power to deal with my Grandparent's business and finance. It was not done so I just wanted to see what was on the table upon her death. My grandmother returned to Huntington mid-1975. She completed her Will and told me to find an apartment in Fort Smith during the Christmas break. I did and on the twenty-third of January 1977, she died. I soon had the property in Huntington transferred to her children because some were in the process of moving me out if I was still in the house when she died. My aunt who lived in the house took control of everything. Upon her death it went to her children. I offered to buy it back after I paid the past due taxes, and they would not. So I was blamed for losing the property by my cousins, but it was not in my name. This information made me a bad person. I lived with them and took care of my grandparents. When their own children did not call or could not help them, I was there. When others fed us, their children were not aware of that. But when my grandmother got my grandfather's Black Lung check I wrote checks to some of them to help their families out and buy cars. Since that time I have had cousins who do not speak or keep in touch with me. I have had it hard with my family. It hurt me real deep, but I learned from my Grandparents that family can do you in before anyone else. If I kept the money that I spent on those family members, who no longer speak to me, I would have had more to spend on myself.

In 1977, my brother Allen came from Kansas City to live with me in Fort Smith. He stayed about two years. This was the longest time I had been around a brother or sister of mine. We helped each other a lot. Many of his new friends were former students of mine. Many would soon find out that we were siblings. One day I came back to our apartment before he left for work and he had several of his friends visiting him and I walked in, and his friends were shocked. I said hello. Allen told them that I was his older brother. They told him I had been their teacher at Northside. Allen questioned them about my teaching and if I had an attitude from hell with them that he knew I could show, a family trait that he knew well. They said at times I had to use it for some of the guys, would push me to that point, but they made it clear that it was for their good. He left the factory job and worked at a clothing store in the Mall. Again, he would not tell many that he was my brother. Our time together helped us to understand each other, and we built a bond that was needed until he died in his mid-fifties. We both had Cancer at the same time. At times we shared how we were dealing with the sickness. Good mental therapy for us. I still miss him. Allen and I got to know each other more and soon learned that we were more alike than different though not living together in our early years, only to see each other for one week at Christmas time. We had different fathers but the same mother and that was no big deal. They visited us and of course we went to Kansas City together during this period. When he moved back to Kansas City. I missed him very much. My friend Larry had just purchased a house that had a two-bedroom apartment in the back. He told me that he would like me to move into the apartment because it would be cheaper for me, and he needed someone who would take care of the place. I quickly moved and stayed there until I left for

Fayetteville in 1980. He and Susan were starting their family, so I became an instant Uncle. A role that I have to this day. Larry and I met when we were at Community College.

This apartment became a center of many transformations for me that I will share with you starting with the following story. One weekend I heard a knock on the door. I opened the door and there stood Omar, one of my students. He came by to visit. While there he told me that he was having trouble at home, and he felt that he could trust me. We had a long discussion of what was going on. I told him very quickly that I was not going to take sides but would see how I could help all parties involved. He asked if he could stay in my second bedroom, I said NO!! I told him to go back home and see if both parties could resolve the problem. I made it clear that I may be breaking a policy for a student staying with me since he was not a family member. He continued to come to class each day and we did not talk about it at school. One day after class I left my classroom for restroom break. Upon returning for the next class Omar's Dad was standing at my door. We greeted each other. He asks me if Omar had moved in with me. I said NO. He told me that his friends were saying that he was at my place. I did tell him that he came by and discussed the idea of moving to my place. I told Omar to go back to them and work it out if possible. His Dad said that he and his wife would talk to Omar and see what could be worked out so all parties would have a clear understanding if it got to that point. I assured his dad that I would under no circumstances take on their parental responsibility. The time came when they asked me to come for dinner. After dinner they approached me and said that Omar could move in with me until the problem was resolved. I said ok to us working this out as a friend of the family to avoid any rumors that may arise. I asked them not to tell many, if anyone, about our agreement. I made it clear that both parents could visit at any time, ensuring that he was living in a safe place. Omar was given money by them to help with my expenses and his expenses. He moved in and he completed high school. His parents addressed the living arrangement with the school when they were asked about it. It was made clear that I was a family friend helping them out with their son who felt that he could not live under their roof, and that he was in a safe place. After graduation he got a job and moved in with a friend to their own apartment. I guess you can say Omar was my "Foster Son" until this day. He is married and has three children.

Then came Ray. He was introduced to me by a mutual friend of ours. He too showed up looking for a room to rent. I needed help with expenses. He got a job and helped around the apartment. He and Omar met each other and became friends as well. Ray married and moved to Tulsa, but that did not work so he returned to my place and stayed in the apartment after I left for Fayetteville. He and his new roommate later moved to a small town in Oklahoma. I lost contact with him for a long time. When I asked a mutual friend in Fort Smith one time if he knew where Ray was, he told me that he got sick and died of an illness. I did not believe that story, but I had no way of finding out through other sources. I told Omar what I heard, and we both could not accept that story.

During an Annual Conference of the United Methodist Church in Fort Smith the friend that told me about Ray's death was at the same conference. I was a delegate from my church in Fayetteville as well as a committee chair. One evening between a business session and Ordination Service I stopped at a convenience store to get a drink and a sandwich. The young man at the counter looked like someone I knew but I couldn't believe what I saw and who it was. It was Ray for sure. He noticed that I was in shock and speechless. I told him that I was told several years ago that he had died of an illness. Ray was told that I got involved with women and got married therefore I stopped communicating with them and they had no contact information for me. It was the person at the conference that I just left told me about Ray's death. Ray and I hugged each other and cried. I could not attend the services because I was not well. We talked between customers until it was time for him to close the store. I returned to my hotel room and could not sleep. The next day I called Omar to tell him about what I experienced the night before. He was not well. I told him where he was working but to date, he had not contacted Ray. I have lost contact in the meantime with Omar as well. But Ray and I talked this week. Omar and Ray were very important in my past and one day all three of us will be together again.

I concluded that I needed a balance between areas I just told you about. So, after a time I felt that more community participation would be that balance. I took to my Leadership skills and my love for politics. My Cousin Curtis Feimster was elected to the Huntington City Council and later elected as the First Black Mayor of a White majority populated town in Western Arkansas. Before his death he held that office for eighteen years. A position came open for the City of Huntington to appoint a person to serve on the Crawford and Sebastian Counties Development Council. I was appointed to that position. Also, I was appointed to the Bi-County Head Start Program. Head Start was one of the Great Society programs of President Johnson. This early year age nutritional program for low-income children gave me the opportunity to assist many families. I worked as the Chairperson of the Policy Sub-Committee and later promoted to the Chair of the Board of Directors. I was there for many years before moving to Fayetteville.

One thing that I was able to do was to help the City of Huntington get grants from the State to install a city-wide water system and put natural gas on the west side of town. During that period, the Mansfield Gas Company who provided gas for the Eastside of town was asking the Public Service Commission of Arkansas for an increase in rates. I had read in the local newspaper about that request. I told Curtis that I would make some calls as a member of the Development Council to the Governor's Office. So, I made a call to his office. I spoke with Governor Bumpers directly since we knew one another and had worked together on the State Democratic Party. I detailed for him the history of the Mansfield Gas Company and why they did not install natural gas on the Westside. The reason was that it was hard to put the line under the bridge leading to Westside. Within weeks I received a call from the Governor Office while at Northside. I went to the Office and was told the call was from the Governor himself. He asked if I could attend a meeting with the Chair of the Public Service Commission the following week. I said yes and I called the commissioner and scheduled that meeting. I and Mayor Curtis's father's uncle, Glenice Feimster, went to Little Rock the next Friday. Uncle Glenice could give detailed information about the situation with the Mansfield Gas Company and the City of Huntington. Some time had passed before I heard from the Commission. Mr. Pat Moran, the Chair of the Commission, said that it was agreed that the Mansfield Gas Company would be granted that rate increase when they could outline how the gas company would install a natural gas line on Westside. I later got news that the water system grant for the city was approved. So, the gas company would put the lines for the water and gas side by side. My grandparents' house got the first water meter because of what I did for the city. Also, while of the Development Council a new wing was built onto the City Hall for our Senior Citizens activities and services to that population. I was honored by the city that I could use the Center as well.

After moving to Fort Smith, I was asked to join the Fort Smith Jaycees. The Jaycees is a leadership training and civic organization for people between the ages eighteen to forty. The Fort Smith chapter was the first in the State of Arkansas, established on May 4, 1936. One of its earlier presidents was the grandson of Judge Isaac C. Parker. I was later elected as first vice president of the chapter. This office allowed me to attend the State Jaycees monthly meetings in North Little Rock. The Fort Smith Chapter nominated me to be a state vice president candidate. I ran for the office and won the office of Vice President for Governmental Affairs. Each year I gained support from several Northwest Jaycees chapters. Each State Convention was full of fun, food, and Purple Passion to drink a toast to everything. I won more elections until I aged out, I think, in 1976. I was named as an "Outstanding Young Man of America" by their Board of Director. I was named again in 1990. During my time in the Arkansas Jaycees, I was named as "One of the Top Four Young Men in Arkansas." I received several State and National level awards as well. In my role as Governmental Vice President, I put together a Jaycees State Legislature Session in the Arkansas House Chamber. I attended other such groups for the Jaycees in Kansas, Oklahoma, and Missouri.

My Grandmother told me at the last Christmas Parade she took me too that I would be grown before I went to another. At that parade, I ran after Santa Claus for three blocks before she caught me. She was up in age. I shared this event to tell you that the next Christmas Parade I can remember attending was when I chaired the parade sponsored by the Fort Smith Jaycees that year. Because of chairing the parade that year I had to do many T.V. and radio shows on the local stations. After that I was asked to do more T.V. noon shows on various topics. I became a regular you might say. When Channel Five went from an ABC station to a CBS station, the Noon Show host stopped by my classroom at Northside and introduced me to the President of CBS. I don't know why but he did. Later I appear at Channel 40 the ABC station on its Noon Show and later was employed by the station to be the camera man at night and on the weekends. That camera experience was only a start for I will have the opportunity to be in front of the camera and not behind the camera.

    As I end this chapter, I can say it was the hardest to write at this point. Maybe it was because I had to reach deeper into my memories and recall certain situations that are still hard to handle.

Chapter 7 — Six Twenty-Nine North Lindell

For the next twenty years I either walked or drove past Old Main, the landmark of the University of Arkansas in Fayetteville. Activities in this landmark and around its campus have given to the State of Arkansas and the United States of America its leaders from all levels of life. I, like so many, had classes in that building. I can recall my experiences when on the campus and walking the halls of Old Main. At times, I felt that my spirituality was tested, such as the day that the elevator stopped between floors for a period. On that sunny day the lights would flash off making the room totally dark.

The person who delivered timber to build the structure was a Black person by the name of Aaron "Rock" Van Winkle. A few weeks ago, I was talking about what I thought about Old Main during my documentary on Van Winkle.

I was also working on campus across from Old Main when the building was closed for safety reasons. The people of Arkansas and former students donated money to restore the building. A very successful campaign. I was there the day Gov. Clinton reopened the building to carry out its mission to the City, State, and the World. I was on campus two weeks ago going through books that contained personal papers in my collection at the Library Special Collection Department I stopped in front of that grand old building. Again, I felt a spiritual experience like I had many times before while on campus.

I cannot talk about Old Main without going across the sidewalk and sharing with you my experience working in the Student Development Center which was the Law School that admitted its first Black student Silas

Herbert Hunt in 1948. I worked in that building for nineteen years. That building, like Old Main, had a spiritual effect on my life. The programs I work for in that building played a major role in my future. But before I started working in that building, I took some time off from taking classes and regrouping mentally and financially. I got a job with the Fayetteville Public Schools at a local Junior High School. That experience would give me the opportunity to apply for a full-time job after completing my Masters. That job lasted for about a year; I think.

When I returned to Fayetteville in 1980, I got a room at the International House, 629 N Lindell where I lived during my Senior year of undergraduate school. This place became the center of my new life. Mrs. Florence Williams was the landlady. She was a retired high school teacher herself. She asked me to work for her by taking on some managing duties of all three of her International Houses and other rental properties. Therefore, I got free rent for working for her. That way I could keep my money from the school job and what little money I had in the bank. What a great deal I had. I also was her driver taking her to the store and shopping duties. Also, when she stopped driving, I would go to the Continuing Education Department to pick up her Independent Course papers each week as well as return them as well.

Mrs. Williams was in some ways ahead of her time by interacting with students from around the world. She gave them a place to stay when many could not stay on campus. Living among them gave me a great insight as I came to know students that came from families from countries in Africa, Europe, Asia, and the Middle East. We became friends and I learned so much about their home and family lives. We talked about the political framework and conflicts that were building up during that period.

One particular case or situation comes to mind. Two of my residents stayed in one of the houses and were on the opposite side politically back home. One day I went to clean up and I opened the ice box and I always passed out due to the smell. What happens is one of the people moved their food into another ice box from the other person from his hometown and a few days later I opened that ice box. Meat and all the food had rotted. I had to tape the door until I had it removed.

I lost contact with many of them when they returned home. Some married Americans in Fayetteville in order to change their visa status. Many paid a lot for that change.

One day one of the students living in the house where Mrs. Williams and I lived told me that he had not seen Mrs. Williams but had heard her in her little room off the main room. I knocked on the door, and I heard no sound. I called out her name but no answer. I opened the door and continued to call out her name and when I entered, I saw her laying there, I could not wake her up, so I made the necessary calls and when the emergency crew arrived the official told me that she had died. I then called her executor and person of contact, and he told me to have her taken to the hospital and then to the funeral home. A Memorial Service was held in a few weeks with only me knowing where she was buried. I remained as the active manager of her property for about two years; the time it took her executor to sell all the rental properties. I was paid again by getting free rent. Also, I was rewarded by taking on all her Continuing Education Courses from 1981-2005 adding High School Sociology and Civics to the list of courses.

Many things happened to me while living at 629 N Lindell that paved the way for so many things in the years to come. It all started with my appearance in the CBS Miniseries The Blue and The Gray. The local TV stations began to report that CBS was coming to

Northwest Arkansas to film a Civil War movie, the area of the State where the Battles of Pea Ridge and Prairie Grove were fought in the 1860s. By having a historical background I knew that I could only be a supply soldier for the North and a Bodyguard or Servant in the Southern Army or be an extra in a group of slaves. You see my Great Great Grandfather Martin was in the Civil War as a Bodyguard for his owner's sons during the war. In 2018 he was honored by the Sons of the Confederacy group with a Cross of Honor placed on his grave at the Family Plot of the Cherokee Chapel Cemetery in Huntington, Arkansas. The only one in any cemetery in the area.

The Blue and the Gray was an epic story of the most explored time of American history. The theme of the movie centered around one family's love that survived it all. The film was based on the works of Pulitzer Prize winner Bruce Catton. That summer I had the honor to meet and be interviewed by his Great Nephew, Ted Catton. Ted was in the area working for the National Park Services at the Pea Ridge Battlefield Park about five miles from my house. Ted was gathering material about the life of Blacks in the area before, during, and after the Civil War. About 6,300 extras were used in the filming of the movie. I later became one of those extras. People stood in long lines to pay five dollars and maybe an audition. I did not have to pay or stand in line. Let me tell you what happened to me.

I was a soloist at Central United Methodist Church in Fayetteville, Arkansas. I happened to do a special the Sunday before the filming of the movie started. A few days later I got a call from the movie company asking me to come for an interview for a part in the movie. During the interview, the producer and several members of the crew commented on my solo and my introduction to the song at church that Sunday. I like to think that I did my audition that Sunday. Two other members of the church had screen time in the final production of the movie.

When I was called for a shooting, it began early in the morning and lasting for about twelve hours most days. I would not know what part I would be in until I got to the warehouse that day. I was in several scenes, mainly in the crowd. One was in a group of Northern supply soldiers. In the crowd scene when Lincoln made a speech during train stop on his way to Washington, D.C. after his election. I was seen on the screen during the shoot later as the doorman at the famous Willard Hotel in D.C. which was my longest time on screen in the movie. I was in the front row of the crowd during the Gettysburg Address. To be that close to Gregory Peck as President Lincoln, I put myself into the event as if I was there in real time. At one point President Lincoln stopped the taping and ask that a group of students watching that day to take off their jackets for the bright colors was a detraction for that period. Also, a lady began to cough and that did not go over too well. She was sent back to the bus. That was the last time I was called back.

Open night came to Springdale, Arkansas on November 14, 15, 16, 1982. All the extras were given free passes to attend. When I saw myself at the Williard Hotel I said out loud "that is me!" In 1984, A movie titled A Soldier's Story was filmed at Fort Chaffee in Fort Smith, Arkansas. I was called for that movie, but I could not do it because I was working full time at the University of Arkansas. I have not forgotten that experience.

After my movie debut I felt that I must return to my studies. I met with Dr. Vizzer, one of my history professors. We had a long talk about my future in huh history. I could be open with her for I trusted her very much. She ensured me that I was brighter than my grades showed in her department. I mentioned that I felt that some of the other professors were prejudiced and would never give me credit and would block me from getting my Masters in that department. We came to the agreement that I would investigate Sociology. Since I had taught it for eight years at the high school level it would be easier for me in that department. The faculty seemed to be more welcoming. I soon learned that sociology would better fit my personality and how to better interact with others. I soon developed a "self" that best fit my values, beliefs, and spiritual growth. Also, I took advantage of the Student Union and the library as my field of studying and observing of society, and to apply sociological theory at other locations. A new me was in the making. My classes were interesting and enjoyable. My teachers were outstanding, and quite helpful.

I began to see my world through what I called my sociological lens. In other words I could see things by zooming in closer to my surroundings or by using a wide-angle lens to see the big picture from a broader context. My research became better as I prepared reports, and papers. What I thought were conflicts and barriers became a challenge that ingrained a better understanding of who I was and could become as I continued a more advanced study of sociology. My interactions with others were more focused on what I had to offer and what they had to offer as well. It became clear that I would stay in Northwest Arkansas, so I began to be more active in my church and within the community.

One day while I was on campus, I saw an announcement for a Part-time Position at the Student Development Center for a counselor for students that were placed on Academic Probation. I applied for the position and was hired. My job was to advise those students and provide study skills and survival skills once they were back in college. I was to monitor their progress and have regular meetings with them during the time of probation. I taught a class on learning skills such as time-management, note-taking, textbook reading, critical thinking, how to set and achieve goals, and other skills. I was their support when they felt things were falling apart. Through this process we became close and built a trusting relationship. Each student had to make a 2.00 grade average at the end of the semester. If that happened, they would be readmitted back in school. I cannot recall my caseload. By the end of that semester, I had a ninety percent success rate. What about those who did not make the required grade point average to return to school? Tony was a football player for the University who did not make the grade point. He told me that he had to return to his hometown of Warren, PA. His dad drove to Fayetteville, AR to take him home. Tony's dad called me to ask for my ideas to get him back into school the next semester. I suggest Independent Courses. He took the required courses and returned the next semester. He changed his major and he went on to graduate with a higher-grade point. Today I received a copy of his first book on Strength and Conditioning. Even today many of those students are in contact with me on a regular basis. Many went on to become mayors of their hometowns, lawyers, educators, owners of their own businesses and of course great parents. We worked together to insure a positive attitude toward life.

    This job also gave me better self-assurance. I called this my entrance into my deep life. I became more stable and spirit centered. I came to understand this new life and put aside negative past instances and build upon a more positive future for me. New doors began to open. My mental state was adjusted for I looked up to the sky and not to the ground. I began to see where I was going. At the end of this I got a new position working for the Student Support Services Program a Government Grant Program from the U.S. Department of Education.

It is now 1984. My part-time position at the Student Development Center was coming to an end. The Director of Student Support Services asked if I would like to do the same thing but with students who were in her program? I told her that I would if the grant was renewed. The program grant was renewed and I started to work for this program in 1984.

The Higher Education Act of 1965 created three educational programs in the U. S. Department of Education (Upward Bound, Talent Search, and Student Support Service known as Trio). I have worked in Student Support Services and the Upward Bound Program for a total of thirty years. The Student Support Services (SSS) program provides support services to low-income students, first generation college students (neither parent received a bachelor's degree), and disabled students enrolled in post-secondary education programs. The goal of the SSS program is to increase the college retention and graduation rates of its participants and help students make the transition from one level of higher education to the next. Grants are rewarded through a grant competition process and funds are awarded to institutions of higher education for a four to five-year grant period.

All SSS programs must provide academic tutoring, which may include instruction in reading, writing, study skills, mathematics, science, and other subjects. They must advise and assist in postsecondary course selection and how to apply for admission to graduate and professional programs, assist students with information about financial aid. The SSS projects may also provide individualized counseling for personal, career, and academic information. I added other assistance such as mentoring the students and providing information if the student needed to work with area Social Services. I had a caseload of one hundred students.

My success rate was at least ninety-five percent in retention and graduating from college. I recall that on many occasions I went to the residence halls of those students who had missed appointments to check on them. I would have lunch in their dining hall and eat with them. For those living off campus I would take a morning or afternoon and ride several buses and if they got on the bus, I would invite them to join me, and we would talk until their stops. Each of these interactions was counted as a contact. If the student worked at a store or eating place I would show up. Each student had to give me information about where they lived or worked. This success rate was not reached because everything worked out without problems and personality crisis between me and the student. I can say that this job was a challenge for me but a great experience. One of my students became my boss for the last three years working for SSS. We talk and visit each other on a regular basis.

At this point in time things were running very well. I felt more at ease and my confidence was coming back, I continued working full-time, attending class, studying for exams and researching to gather resources for my papers. A new pathway was in sight. One day I was talking to another staff member. He mentioned that he worked on the weekend at a local radio station in Fayetteville. He explained his duties as producer of a talk show hosted by a Professor in the College of Education discussing educational topics relevant to the present-day issues in American Education. As we talked, he said to me that the host of that talk show needed a co-host to work with him and could be available if he had to miss a program. The staff member said that I should schedule a meeting with the host to see what he was looking for in a co-host position. The next week I met with the host, and we came to an agreement that he was willing to try it with me. Again, a new door was opening for me.

I was very nervous when I got to the station on Saturday. The first day I just listened to the show to get a feel. The show was for two hours, and the time went quickly. Each time we did the show I became more comfortable. Before long a year had gone by doing the show.

I can recall that the owner of the radio station would come into the studio and listen to us. This did not bother me, but he showed concern in what we were doing, and our topics were in line with the station's purpose and goal within the community. One Saturday after the program went off the air and the other host had left the station I was talking to the producer and the owner came into the production studio. He spoke to the both of us. He then asked me to come with him into the studio and that he would like to talk with me. That was a surprise, and we went into the studio. He looked at me and said that he liked the way I discussed the topics, how well I was working with the other person, and I was very knowledgeable of the subject matter. He looked at me and said, "If I can get a sponsor would you be willing to do your own show on Sunday afternoons for two hours?" I was speechless for a few seconds. I said, really? It would take about two weeks to work it out and I could start the first Sunday of next month. He would arrange everything with the other host for the transition. My preparation had begun. I had to select a theme for the show. Topics that would spark interest, how would I promote the show, who would be my focus audience's and what would they be interested in and how I will get them to share in the discussion engaged for two hours each week.

The deal was put together and I got paid each week for each show. I came up with a name, "Moore Talk." I had a theme song that I played at the start and ending of each show "Tear of Joys" by Allen and Allen. The name for the show and the intro music assisted me in defining the concept of the show. The format of the show was to have invited guests who would share their insight though the skill of talking with the host and addressing any questions from the audience who called in to share their ideas with the guest. I began to brainstorm to decide my topics to invite the right experts with the necessary expertise. I used my education and life expenses for topics that would build up each other from week to week. When I offered an invitation, I would engage with each guest what I had in mind and how their personality and knowledge would fit the topic of discussion and how comfortable it would make them to share with unknown audiences.

I made it a point to make sure that the audience would return the next week. I would share with them the topic for the next week before leaving the air. I would also give a one liner about the guest. The producer made announcements doing the week and especially the day before.

What made my show so important were the topics, just to list a few of them:
1) Who Am I or Think That I Am?
2) Facing the American Dream.
3) We Must Experience Our Own Spirituality.
4) How to Select the Right Career.
5) The Art of Being a Mid-wife.
6) A Tribute to Black Women in The Arm Forces.
7) Generation X.
8) Our Youth of Fayetteville.
9) How to Express Your Grief.
10) Role of The National Rifle Association in American Society.

This is only a small list of all the shows I had. I can't recall the total number because I did not start out recording each show but in my Personal Collection at the University of Arkansas Special Collection Department I have about thirty tapes and scripts of shows.

The show ended because too many of my shows were pre-exempted by University of Arkansas Baseball games on Sundays and other events during the year. The station owner told me that KHOG Radio made me the first and only Black talk show and host in Northwest Arkansas. I thanked the owner for giving me that great opportunity and was honored to be the first and only of my race in Northwest Arkansas to share with the community the various views of society that many had never experienced. So, I returned to my normal life and finished my master's degree.

Chapter 8 — Upward Focus

From 2003 -2014 I was the Director of the Upward Bound Program at Northwest Arkansas Community College (NWACC) in Bentonville, Arkansas. Our first grant was awarded during the 2003 Grant Competition Period. The grant was for two hundred sixty thousand dollars per year for four years.

What is Upward Bound? The program provides fundamental support to participants in their preparation for college entrance. The program provides opportunities for participants to succeed in their precollege performance and, ultimately, in their higher education pursuits.

Upward Bound serves high school students from low-income families, and high school students from families in which neither parent holds a bachelor's degree.The goal of Upward Bound is to increase the rate at which participants complete secondary education and enroll in and graduate from institutions of postsecondary education.

All Upward Bound projects provided instructions in math, laboratory science, composition, literature, and foreign language. Each program is to inform the parents and students of the Federal Student Financial Aid Program and benefits that would help high school seniors to enroll into a Community College or University after Fall or Spring graduation. We had one hundred percent graduation rate each year we had our Grant.

By working part-time at NWACC as a Sociology Instructor, I was told by the Dean of Student Affairs that the college was applying for the Upward Bound Grant. I was encouraged to apply for the Director's Position. I was happy at the University of Arkansas in Student Support Services, but I did apply and was given an interview. The interview was more about educating the committee members about Trio and how it would help the college in many ways. I had to give them some insight into me, and how I would be a good fit for the college. I even dressed in the college colors. A few weeks later I got a call and was offered the Directorship of the new Upward Bound Program. I went back and read our Student Support Services grant since the program objectives for both Programs were formatted similarly. I had to put together a staff that would include an Academic Coordinator, Administrative Assistant, Instructors for our classes, and build a relationship with the target school Counselors and Staff. But most of all, building trust and a strong relationship with the students and parents is very important.

I would stay at the University until the end of the summer of 2003. I could not leave my staff there without helping with the summer orientation sessions. My boss at the University did not know that I had applied for another job, let alone getting it and I couldn't leave her hanging with the summer orientation coming on in a few months. My job at NWACC started on September 1, 2003.

I felt that this transition was an advancement in my career. I did not leave the University because I did not have a good relationship with my co-workers. My relationships were good with most of the people I worked with. At times I had to deal with those who were over our Program that made it clear that I would not get a promotion if they were assigned to our Program. My biggest blockers came from other Black administrators. As a student at the University in the 1970s I was not a part of the inner Black student group, mainly because of how I was raised. I was raised in a diverse community in Western Arkansas that responded differently from those of other parts of the state. My relationship with the white students and staff was not racially motivated as it was for those from other locations in Arkansas.

So, when it was time to be the Director of the Upward Bound Program, going to mainly White schools was something I had no problems with. My communications skills were also a positive trait that worked well for me, and I organized the operation of the Upward Bound Program. The Grant did outline the process in developing a strong program. These components of the Grant included a statement of need, objectives, a plan of operation, school support, quality personnel, an evaluation plan, and of course a budget. My first official job was to hire a staff which included an Academic Coordinator, an Administrator Assistant, instructors, tutors, van or bus driver for our students in the outlining schools of Bentonville. Following these duties it was time to put together visits to the target schools to have discussions with the counselors to set up a timetable to have our introductory sessions with the students that might be eligible for the program. Before these general sessions I asked the counselors to look at students that met government requirements as low-income families, neither parent graduated with a four-year college degree, and those who had at least a two-point grade average and had a good conduct record and with low attendance rate. Each student was given an application supplied by the Counselor to be completed by parents, an information package for the parents and an evaluation for the Counselor to complete as well for each student they would recommend. I would return to the school in a week or two to gather the information to move on to the rating process. At the end of the recruitment process we had our first eighty-five new Upward Bounders that were eligible for the program. During each visit I had a meeting with the principal if available.

    Our staff was breaking new ground for the college. We needed a program based more around the culture and educational traits of the students and parents, and not like the University's Upward Bound Program.

Before we put our program in operation many meetings were held in the schools and with the parents to set the foundation and ensure that all were on the same level of thinking. It was made clear that our program would treat all students on an equal basis. Our staff would work together to build a sense of trust and understanding in dealing with the students and parents. Joint decisions would be based on consensus. As Director I would make sure that I was in charge to implement the grant based on the guidelines in the Grant and what the U.S. Department of Education demanded. Federal Grants requirements and guidelines were not the same that were used by the State or even the institution that received the Grant. For example, I would oversee the Budget expenses and not the Business Office Director but would work with them to see that all expenses were spent for the right line item in the budget. After each National Trio Conference I would make sure that the Financial Officer of the College was updated with the latest guidelines dealing with the regulations and rules of what we could or could not use our funds as outlined in the Grant. The Upward Bound staff would be a part of the College personnel to promote the goals and objectives of the College to ensure community building. When we traveled, we would be representing the College at its highest level of respect.

I feel that it is not important for you to hear about the technical operation of the Grant but what affect did this program have on the cultural and educational development of the student and how we prepared them to continue their education beyond high school. More of our students enjoyed the program and stayed in the program until graduation from high school. One reason that more stayed was how our staff showed no differences between the students or the family background of students. We made sure that the Parents got to know each other by having them to meet and our staff would talk to them by giving them monthly progress reports. If a problem or situation happened, we had a meeting with both the students and the parents. A peaceful solution was reached, and we all moved on to the next level. By having this cooperation things moved smoothly.

If a situation became a conflict or to be better explained the staff moved quickly to readjust the matter. This may have included rules for the trips, hotel room assignments, conduct while in the hotel, while shopping and at mealtimes on the trips, or other situations that needed to be told to the parents and others going on the trip. It was important to make sure that everyone knew our stand on all issues that might arise. At one parent meeting a new parent asked, "How do I know that my child will be safe on this trip." Another parent, quickly said, "I have pictures sent to us of Mr. Moore sitting outside in the hallway on the boys' floor at midnight and at one time two A.M. according to the time that the picture was sent." To enforce our rules, our staff made it clear that if their child became a problem or got an item that they did not pay for and got caught by the authorities the Parent would have to come and get the student or make arrangements to get them home for the student would not delay the trip in any way and would not return on the bus if the situation occurred beyond one hour of home. The staff did not have to deal with this situation at any time. Each trip was fun and enjoyable and a cultural experience for all. On many of these trips our instructors were invited to continue their teaching moment by making the trip a field exercise. One of our instructors was also a parent of three of our students as well. She became our Mother in Residence and one of our van drivers each day for the area she lived in that had other students that she could transport to all events.

We had to build trust, have confidence in these students, and they realized that it was a stepping stone for them in giving them a future that they wouldn't have had. These students went places and did things that I did or didn't have the opportunity to do, for I made it a point to make that a focus point. I did share with them that when I was their age, I could not go to many places for they were often for Whites only. So, on each trip I made the students interact with each other and not just those from their schools. The few Black students in the program had to interact with the others as well. This group exhibited this togetherness publicly. I can recall a lady asking me on one of the trips if this was a church group of teenagers? I told her about our program and what we did at the end of our summer program. She left with a smile on her face, telling me that this group gave her hope for a better future in the country. I shared the discussion with the group when we got back on the bus.

But I must tell you that the staff had disagreements but did our best not to react in front of the students, all but once, and it showed them that the staff were human, and we had to work on our attitudes as well. I was aware of some of the habits the staff had and would do away from the students, but I did not let the staff know it for I too have habits that I had to control for things to work out for the betterment of students. It taught them something about being human and that we were not perfect. The staff did their best to mention to our instructors that these were high school students and not the college students that they taught. We did lose some instructors because that had trouble relating to some of our students. The school Counselor shared with us concerns they had about our students and their conduct when in school and other situations related to home life that we needed to know. It is true that we had many happy and productive outcomes that the college administration felt insecure about in the beginning. College staff and administration were invited to our events and an open invite at any time we had classes and events on campus.

Our year-end trips were our way of rewarding our students. Our first-year end trip was to Kansas City since it was our first one and closer to home. Since my mommy and family lived in Kansas City, I knew the places to visit that would be educational, and with some fun included. We visited the Truman Library there and museum that had cargo from a ship that sunk in the Kansas River many years ago. We went to other places in the area including a visit to the Mayor's Office because he was a friend of mine. This was the first time many of the students had been on a Charter Bus and had stayed in a nice Hotel overnight. All expenses were paid of course.

Our Presidential Library trips (Eisenhower, Johnson, Jackson, Lincoln, Clinton, and Truman) were both fun and educational. We took enough pictures to fill two instant cameras on each trip. The most modern library with special effects was the Lincoln Library and visiting his tomb was eye opening to each of us. The Johnson Library was special in that Mr. Johnson was the President who established the Upward Bound Program. We also went to the Johnson Ranch that connected his life to our mission.

Many times on these trips we would include a university or college that would give our Seniors avenues to continue their education. We visited the Universities of Texas, New Mexico, Nebraska, to name a few. Many of our Seniors were given offers to attend some of the schools we visited. In the life of our program all our Seniors graduated from high school and went on to attend many of our largest schools of higher education outside of the State of Arkansas, and within the State as well. Our Senior graduation rate for each year that we had a graduation class was one hundred percent. We assisted our students with their application, ACT, and financial forms. All that were accepted got all expenses paid at the school for four years. It was because our staff worked together with the high schools and parents.

    Not all their time was centered around academics, as there were family and personal situations many of the students were dealt with. One story I cannot forget. I had a student that was to have a child while in the program. She asked if she had to drop out of the program. After talking with my staff and the school I told her no. From that point forward we made no difference in her and the other students. She needed our help more than ever. One day in a private meeting with me she told me that she was taken out of a garbage can in Mexico by a couple who heard her crying. The couple took her home and raised her. She said to me that she wanted to have her child so that child would not be in a garbage can like her. The last time I saw her was in the Counselor's Office at the high school checking on her graduation status since we made sure she stayed in school and graduated. While she was in the counselor's office, I held the baby who was a few weeks old. When she came out of the meeting we hugged and that was the last time I saw her and the baby, some fifteen years or more.

    About four months ago while out eating at my favorite restaurant this young man came out of the kitchen to get a drink. As he returned to the kitchen he looked toward our table. He went into the kitchen to return shortly and came to our table and said hello to me. He told me that he was in my Upward Bound Program many years ago and he told me his name that I did remember, and he thanked me for getting him the money to continue his education to be a Chef. He invited me to his new job here in town. I cannot wait to go and have him prepare me a meal. I later was told by his boss and my friend that he shares how he knew me and how I helped with his career that led him to that restaurant. Last night I had the opportunity to dine at the restaurant where the student was the Chef. The meal he prepared I would put on the same level of food I have had at the White House, and other high-class restaurants I have eaten at in my life. To my surprise the meal was on him, so I gave our server a good tip.

I had a student whose mother was very ill. He had to sleep in or near her room at night. He shared with me the situation and said that he may not be able to go on the year-end trip because of her condition. She called me one day and told me that she was getting worst, and it is not long for her death was near. I prayed with her, and we talked a little while longer. She asked me to see after her Son. She told me that his aunt was coming to live with them and see after him until he finished high school. I said I would as long as I could. She died a few weeks later and when he went to the funeral home to pick up her ashes, he asked me to go with him and his family. I did and it meant so much to him. After graduation he moved to Chicago to live with another relative, went to college and graduated. We talked or wrote to each other many times a year for about ten years. One day he called and mentioned to me that he was applying for a new job, and he wanted to use me as a reference. I agreed, and a person called and did an interview over the phone. He was applying for a job with the U.S. Department of the Treasury. The lady called back within weeks and told me that he got the job, and it was because of me and the promise I had made to his mother that led the Department to hire him. I made my call yesterday to check on him. He is doing great.

When I had cancer the students and staff were there for me. I had to have radiation treatments each afternoon for a total of forty-five. I would walk across the street from the College for treatments then return to work. I missed no days while taking treatments. I could go on trips if it was at the weekend when there were no treatments. Each evening after work I would go home, eat dinner and go to bed. The students and staff gave me encouragement and kept my spirits up during this time.

I owe so much to them. But at the end of that summer program 2009 I could not go on the Summer Trip because I had to have two more radiation treatments. The support I had during that time helped me to make a full recovery and I continued as Director for five more years.

My work in the United Methodist Native American Ministry gave me connections with the Native American Community and its Culture. Also, my own Native American lineage led me to offer a summer course for my Upward Bound student called Basic Sioux Language Class. My friend Rev. Joe Brown Thunder from the Standing Rock Reservation of South Dakota came to NWACC, Bentonville to teach a six-week class on his language and culture. These students I'm sure were the only ones who could speak in the Sioux language in Northwest Arkansas. At the end of summer the students sang for the students, staff, instructors and Board Members of NWACC; How Great Thou Art in Sioux. So our Year End Trip was to visit Joe Brown Thunder's home in South Dakota for two days, then on to see Mount Rushmore, Crazy Horse Mountain, The Badlands, and on to Yellowstone National Park for three days. I know I could have added other stories, but these provided insight to the importance of programs like this one for our disadvantaged students in Northwest Arkansas surrounding the World of Walmart.

In 2014 it was time for me to retire and hand things to a younger staff member to be Director for the last two years of the Grant cycle. Things were changing in the educational system therefore our new student's mindset began to conflict with my way of doing things. I felt a younger staff mindset would relate more with them. I had over thirty years of Trio and that was enough for me. In the 2017 Grant Cycle, the NWACC Reapplication was rejected for not following the page limit requirements and other complicating factors. Northwest

Arkansas Community College had not reapplied for a grant since 2017.

I concluded that this part of my life story should end with my retirement even though I stayed on at the college as a part-time Sociology instructor until March of 2023.

Chapter 9 — The Person I See in the Mirror

This book is about how I, as an individual, gained a sense of who I am or in other words, self. This is one sociological theory that I have taught to my students since 1972, as a teacher at Northside High School, in Fort Smith, Arkansas. The sociological approach became a connection point from my car accident in 1952 to the present day. This is a complex concept (Charles Horton Cooley, "looking-glass self"). Cooley (1909) believed that we all act like mirrors to each other, reflecting to one another an image of ourselves. We do this by using three steps:

1. We imagine how we look to others.
2. We imagine other people's judgment of us.
3. We experience feeling about ourselves based on our perception of other people's judgments.

A long time ago I decided that I would do my best to be that person that I see each day in the mirror, the same person that other people see. Along the way my mirror was fogged over so that I could not see a clear reflection of myself. But why did that happen? It could be that I was not seeing the person that I should have been at that time, or a situation had caused that fog to overshadow the view. We may display a faulty image around others and the true self never come through. At times as I interacted with others or within a group, I was not comfortable with my surroundings or the individual I was standing near. For years I was self-conscience of the scar on the left side of my head, that so many people asked what happened. Today it is not as visual as it was when I was younger. I was able to put that to rest because it became no big deal when I met a person who did not know or even care about it or saw it. But it was because of that mark that guided me along the way and kept me grounded in so many ways so that I could do anything, and it would not hold me back to attaining my goals in life. At times when I felt like a failure, I just rubbed the side of head and pushed forward. But most of all I understood early in my life who saved me after my accident, God and Drs. G.G. and Merle Woods, the love of my grandparents and the support I had in my hometown. As I continued my life journey all of those who saw my potential knew that I would be successful. I made a pact that if I could help somebody along the way my living would not be in vain. When I take my last breath on this earth and enter Heaven, I will know that I lived up to that pact.

I strongly think that the self that made me what I am today was centered around my spiritual development in early childhood. Around the age of twelve, known as the age of reason, I began to question things around me and my physical transformation. I can recall this situation that happened to me one day on the way to the neighborhood store for my grandmother. When I went to that store, I would go through the strip pits where they once mined coal behind our house. It was quicker to go that way.

One day on the way to the store I was walking along, at one of the turns of the path was a tall bush. I have passed that bush on many occasions, but that day has I approached that bush it began to shake, I thought that it was a little animal or bird. As I got closer to the bush, I could hear what I thought was a voice, but I looked and saw nothing. I ran on to the store. I did not stay long that day talking to Mr. Columbus, the man at the store, for I had to rush back to the bush to see if I would hear that voice or the bush would shake again. I came upon the bush, and I looked and stood quietly; I heard nothing, and it did not shake. I ran home. I did not tell my grandmother or anyone about what happened that day. I would look out of the bedroom window at night and think about that bush. From that day forward I did not have that experience again.

I began to feel that bush experience was a sign from God about my spiritual need and it was time to be baptized. Soon after that our Sunday School lesson was about Moses and the burning bush. My bush was not on fire, but it did shake. I prayed for weeks about what I should do. I finally told my grandparents and Rev. Perry that I would like to join the church the following Sunday July 3, 1960. On that day I was baptized at the same altar as my great-great grandparents, great grandparents, grandparents, and Mommy. I was the only one of my Mommy's children baptized at that altar. I attended that church on a regular basis until 1977, but I would return for special services.

In 2009, I visited my dear friend Pharaoh, during Christmas. I had known him all my life and he was very nice to me. He taught me many things about nature and plants that I could or couldn't eat in the wild. Also, he taught me footprints of certain animals in the area. He was the first science teacher I had. He was a very good artist, for he would do cartoon cards for people. I did not find out until later in his life that he drew me and on one of my final visits with him he drew one of me sitting next to him. But what came to reality was when he mentions the expression I had on my face the day he shook that bush when I was on the way to the store, he laughs because he thought I knew it was him that day, but I did not. It was then I found out who did it and it was not a spiritual sign. But to me it was a sign that I will never forget. My September 9, 1952, experience had the same impact as the bush toward the self that developed along the way.

I think that spirituality, values, belief system, and faith were factors in the development of my self-image-the person I see in the mirror. Spirituality is how I search for meaning and purpose of life. Values are an enduring belief on how I act, my attitudes, and how I behave to reach a desirable end. A belief system based on a set of principles of what is true that influences my human behavior and perceptions. Faith, the complete trust or confidence in someone or something.

My spiritual journey started at Arnett Chapel African Methodist Episcopal Church in Huntington. Arkansas. It was there that I began to think about why I recovered from my accident to have more years on this earth. From that day I began to understand what life was about and why I am a human being who was not perfect. I soon learned that I would be critical of others and they too me. But as I matured, I became less critical toward others and if they were critical of me, I knew that I must understand why and not react quickly. As I grew older, I had more control over the situation and relied on the fact that I could not answer for them, but just for myself. I had several situations in my life, like all of us, in which it was hard to hold back emotions and reactions. I concluded that is just part of the life of a human being. I can say that I have had many signs that defined the meaning and purpose of life. My interaction with those I encountered at my job, while teaching, many years of church participation, friends, and family are just a few examples.

I would like to state that my values were instilled to me by my grandparents. Because of them I was able to develop my beliefs, my attitude and how my behavior could define who I was and to know the difference between what is right or wrong. This was hard at times. That is why I think of the song, "He Looked Beyond My Faults and Saw My Needs". I soon put into my consciousness that if I did anything that made me feel bad don't do it again, but on the other hand if I felt no guilt do it better the next time. I will be seventy-five years old shortly I still must deal with my values.

When we think of beliefs of what is true, these truths influence our human behavior and perceptions. How I act in each situation is based on previous interactions. Some behaviors are shaped by role models. Many of my role models were good ones. Also, I was very cautious of those who seemed to be fake and seem to be untrustworthy.

When we think of faith, we see it more in the context of religion, which is "belief in God or in the doctrines or teaching of religion." But in context of society faith is complete trust or confidence in someone or something. What is important to me when it comes to faith, how did I gain faith in that person? In the religion context my faith is strong because of belief in God.

My spirituality, values, belief system, and faith, that best reflects a true image of that person in the mirror did not stop when I left Huntington, Arkansas for the Fort Smith area and later to Fayetteville, and now in Bentonville. But as I got more involved in the United Methodist Church beyond the local level these factors had more of a meaning and purpose in my life. You see, my family have been Methodist since the early 1880s. I remember my godmother, Aunt Ruth, who told me in Sunday School, what John Wesley, the founder of Methodism stated, "Do Good, Do No Harm, but stay in love with God." Also, Aunt Ruth said that "we accept people where they are in life at that point, then move them toward perfection because their past is their past." For I think it is wrong to be critical of a person's past because it wasn't my past. I can only be critical of my own past. So many want to go back to the way it was, because we have never done it that way before. There is not a part of my past that I would like to revisit, for it was hard the first time.

While attending Central United Methodist Church in Fayetteville, I was invited to go on a John Wesley Tour of England, that would take me to the places John

Wesley ministered and traveled in England. I told the Pastor, Rev. Jack Wilson that I did not have travel money. He later called me and told me that he was making the final list of those who would be going on the trip and that I would be on that list. I was surprised when he told me that, and that all my expenses would be paid. I never knew for sure who paid for it. I was so surprised that I would be retracing the path of John and Charles Wesley as they established the Methodist movement in England. This tour affected my spirituality and made me a better Christian which provided a better understanding of what it meant to be Methodist. To physically visit Wesley's family home was touching as if it was a real place. Our visit to Stratford upon the River Avon, the birthplace of the world's greatest playwright William Shakespeare, to physical stand on the Stage of the Global Theater where his plays were performed. To see Oxford where John was admitted to study and lead the Holy Club. The Queen of England was present the day our guided tour made the Windson Castle stop. She made her presence known by riding past on her horse.

In Coventry, England we past the filming location of a story where the town tailor Tom, was said to have watched as Lady Godiva rode her horse through the town naked and he looked acquiring the name "Peeping Tom." To sit in John Wesley Chapel and experience that strangely warm feeling. So when I became more active and involved in the ministry of the United Methodist on the World stage that tour comes to mind. The United Methodist Church (UMC) to me is a good example that has given me the opportunity to express and exhibit those factors mentioned above because of its connection that links our Christian beliefs and how we are able to practice them. I think I call this a renewal process.

I would like in the next pages to highlight some achievements in a connectional context by representing the Arkansas Annual Conference on both the Annual and General Church level of the UMC structure from

1993-2016. Native American Ministry Conference Chair (nineteen years), Board Member of Native American Comprehensive Plan (twelve years) Member on the General Board of Church and Society (eight years) and Member on the General Commission on Religion and Race (four years). On the local level, I was a Charter Member of Living Waters United Methodist Church, Centerton, Arkansas (2005 to the present). Each of these boards and agencies had a common effect on my self-image.

Have you ever taken a class in school and college that you enjoyed and knew that you never could use it in your lifetime? One of my history courses in the 1970s was Native American History that was taught by one of the leading authors in the United States on the Native American history and culture. At the 1993 Arkansas Annual Conference of the United Methodist Church had to form a Committee on Native American Ministry (CONAM). As the nomination committee read the list of nominees, they read the Chair of the CONAM would be J. Harris Moore. Many in the room began to laugh, and many said. "Why a Black American?" They did not know that I was a Descendant of Choctaw Freedmen who was on the Trail of Tears. Our responsibility was to determine the distribution of the Native American Ministries Sunday offering taken on the Third Sunday of Easter, coordinate the promotion of Native American Ministries Sunday as a Speaker within Arkansas, and to monitor Native American ministries within the Annual Conference. Since Arkansas did not have a Native American Church, we adopted the Oklahoma Indian Missionary Conference. Related to the CONAM was the Native American Comprehensive Plan. This plan was to enrich United Methodist Native American ministries by developing and supporting existing and new Native American congregation's ministries and fellowship and to affirm the value and strengthen the role of traditional, cultural, and spiritual contribution of Native American people for the expression of Christian faith and faith development among the membership of the Church. I was able to build strong relationship with Native American leader in and out of the Church. These relationships strengthen my own spirituality and faith. I was not an outsider as I travel throughout the Native American Nations or Indian Country. Still today I have that relationship with so many that I worked with for over the past thirty years. This experience has given a spot to work with the United States Senate Committee on Native American Affairs in policy making and decision-making process as well. Singing in the native language, visiting a Reservation in South Dakota, and attending meetings with many Nation Chiefs gave me a different view of that person I see in the mirror.

My work on the General Board of Church and Society contributed again to this spiritual development. I dedicated myself to my living faith as I sought justice and peace within our society. It is this group within the structure of the United Methodist Church that implements the Social Principles (the prayerful and earnest efforts to speak to issues) in the contemporary world from a sound biblical and theological foundation and Methodist tradition and other policies of the Church.

This Board fulfilled the mandate of relating the Gospel of Jesus Christ to the Church, communities, and world in which we live. Also, by bringing the whole of human life into conformity with the will of God. The highlight of working on this Board was the Bioethics Task Force. We were charged to consider a wide range of issues that relate to genetic testing. This guide would develop resources for pastoral and congregational use. The task force was also charged with researching issues related to artificial insemination and other reproductive methods. The task force was guided by Dr. Barbara Lukert and J. Harris Moore along with the General Board staff person Linda Bales Todd. The final report was titled, "Spiritual Discernment: A Guide for Genetic and Reproductive Technologies" (2004) This guide was sent to United Methodist Churches worldwide. This Board had a Church Center for the United Nations in New York City. I served as Vice-Chair of the United Nations Ministry Task Force. While attending a required International Conference representing the United Methodist Church, the Twin Towers were hit and became known ever since as 9/11. That event caused many years of health problems for me because of the smoke and dust in the air that day and those days following before I could leave town.

As I stated earlier in my writing, I was raised in the African Methodist Episcopal Church, a majority Black church that did not have a board dealing with the issue of race in the church. So, when I was asked to represent our Annual Conference on the Board of the General Commission on Religion and Race, I couldn't wait to see how this group functioned. This General Commission on Religion and Race was formed to hold the newly formed United Methodist Church in 1968 accountable in its commitment to reject the sin of racism in every aspect of the life of the church. This group works for its members to realize the possibility of a world where every member of the human family can live, love, and express a sense of freedom and peace. We worked hard to dismantle racial discrimination in all its forms. I began to understand that core values could have a biblical base with a relationship with God and one another. I was able to see how that person I saw in the mirror had a relationship of Love, Grace, Equity, Justice, Respect and Mutual Accountability. Yet today we still have the forces of discrimination and oppression that seek to tear us apart. I saw many congregations that would not promote minorities programs and would not assist in the ministries of those minorities on special Sunday Offering sponsored by the United Methodist Church.

Let me end this chapter and book with this thought, do you recall the first time you looked into the mirror and realized that it was you? I cannot recall. But I do know now that each time I look into a mirror I say to myself, "do others see the same person that I see and express to them the true me?" As you close this book place it where you can see it from time to time and may it be as inspirational to you as it was for me. Today I do know why… I Changed My Name.

Images of My Life

City Flag - Huntington, Arkansas
The colors of the flag (green, yellow, black) inspired the book cover.

*Mr. and Mrs. Lloyd Repass - Fiftieth Wedding Anniversary
"They were my neighbors in Huntington."*

Doyle and Eva Moore
"My Grandparents that raised me in Huntington."

Huntington, Arkansas Post Office, 1952

Edward Harrison - Huntington Postmaster
"'Peanut' was my early mentor."

Dr. G. G. Woods
"He saved my life after the early car accident."

Me and My Sister

My Brothers and Sisters

My birth mother - Darlene

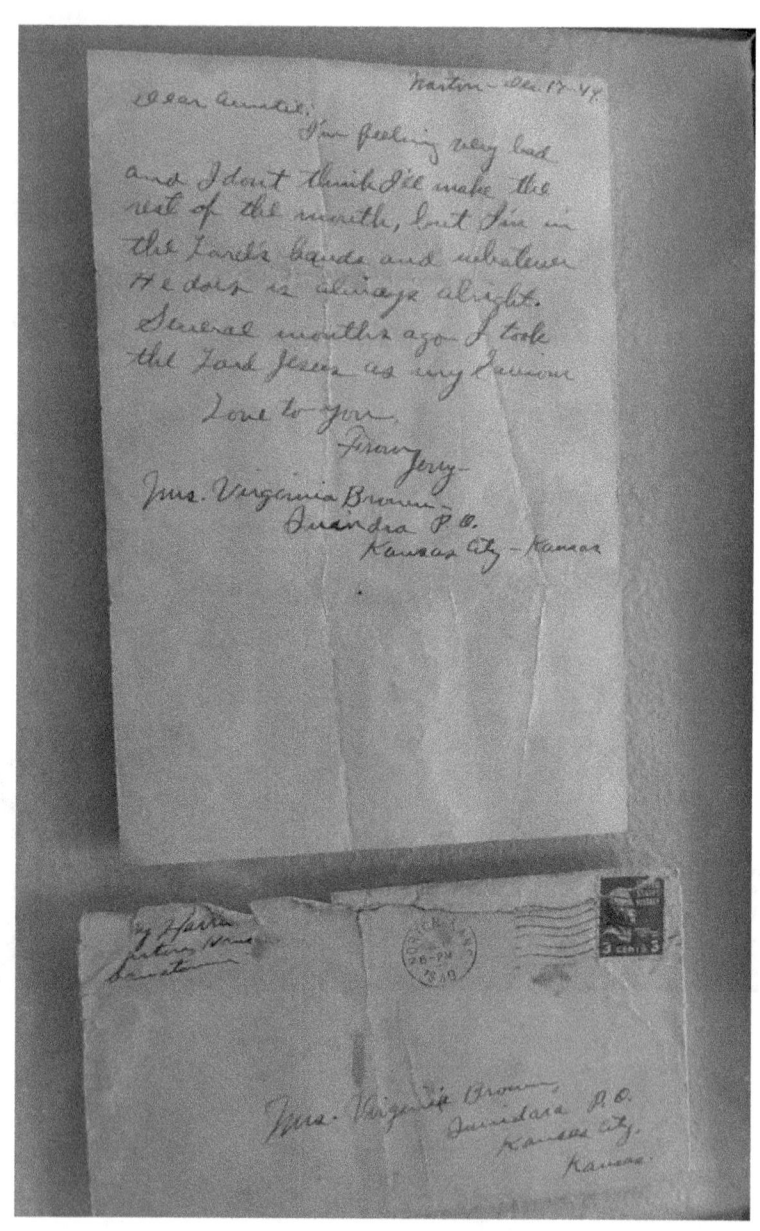

Last letter written to my great aunt from my father Jerry Sr. weeks before he died.

Northside High School - Fort Smith. Arkansas
"My first teaching job."

November 17, 1992

Clinton/Gore '92
P.O. Box 615
Little Rock, AR 72203

Dear Mr. Clinton:

    I didn't know if I could say "Dear Bill" since you are now my friend and the President-elect of the U.S.A. This is how my brother Allen, that lives in Kansas City addressed you, "as my friend, the President-elect" on election night.

    It is now 1:30a.m., November 17, 1992, the date of my Grandmother's 91st birthday if she was still living. This was the lady you met in 1974, while campaigning in Mansfield. After that warm greeting she told me to always support you and I have. I guess that is why I didn't make a big issue when my boss asked for one hour of annual leave to be assessed against my accrued leave time when I only left thirty minutes early for the October 23 Rally at the University of Arkansas. In other words, I had lied about leaving only thirty minutes early. The time deducted was no big deal, but don't call me a liar. Today that same person is asking other if you have offered me a position within your administration. I had to share this because it has been on my mind for several weeks.

    Mr. Clinton, I would like to share with you as a friend these words that I have recalled to help me through those situations mentioned above to take with you to the White House. "Wake up each morning with your mind stayed on Jesus, for He will open doors for you. Doors you are unable to see".

    I thank God for you as a fellow Christian, a friend, a Governor, and a President to be. If I can be of any assistance please write or call me at my office (575-5787).

                                             Sincerely,

                                             Jerry Harris Moore

My Letter to President-elect Bill Clinton

*Autographed photograph from
U.S. Representative John Paul Hammerschmidt*

My High School Yearbook Photograph

Me chillin' (with seldom used pipe).

Me celebrating my life.

My fiftieth birthday when I gave my family papers to the University of Arkansas Special Collection - 1999.

www.ingramcontent.com/pod-product-compliance
Lightning Source LLC
Chambersburg PA
CBHW071120160426
43196CB00013B/2639